INSIGHTS
for
CHRISTIAN LIVING

INSIGHTS
—————— for ——————
CHRISTIAN LIVING

DANIEL L. SEGRAVES

Insights for Christian Living

by Daniel L. Segraves

©1988 Word Aflame Press
Hazelwood, MO 63042-2299

Printed in United States of America.

WORD AFLAME PRESS
pentecostalpublishing.com

Library of Congress Cataloging-in-Publication Data

Segraves, Daniel L., 1946–
    Insights for Christian living.

    1. Christian life—Pentecostal authors. I. Title.
BV4501.2.S414 1988   248.4   88-234
ISBN 0-932581-31-5

Contents

Introduction

The material in this book was written from a pastor's perspective over a period of seven years. It was originally distributed in a newsletter sent to church members and other interested persons.

With the passing of time and a change in my personal ministry from that of pastor to that of training young men and women for the work of God, it became apparent that the essence of the material previously written would be helpful to a wider cross section of the church. To accomplish that purpose, the work has been completely reorganized and condensed.

A grasp of the material in this book will assist the believer in becoming firmly rooted in his Christian experience. It is not a doctrinal work as such. It concentrates instead on the practical aspects of Christian living.

Included are discussions of the importance of thinking right, developing Christian character qualities, successful spiritual warfare, Bible study, the nature of the church, of forgiveness, prosperity and success, church growth, the Christian's civic duty, Christian education, prophecy, and assorted other topics relevant to Christian growth. The last chapter will be of particular interest to preachers.

I express my gratitude to my wife, Judy, for originally having the vision and initiative to put this material in book form. She worked over a period of months to transfer it from the original newsletter format to that of a book manuscript. Without her encouragement and effort, it is doubtful that this book would ever have been completed.

It has been my prayer that God would direct me in the final preparation of the manuscript. If it is helpful to the reader in strengthening his or her footing on the Christian path, I will be amply rewarded for my efforts.

Daniel L. Segraves

1

Thinking Christian Thoughts

M an is a spirit being who lives in a physical body. His spirit nature is made of both the soul and the spirit. For this reason, Paul said, "I pray God your whole spirit and soul and body be preserved blameless unto the coming of our Lord Jesus Christ" (I Thessalonians 5:23).

It is possible to distinguish between the soul and spirit, according to Hebrews 4:12: "For the word of God is quick, and powerful, and sharper than any twoedged sword, piercing even to the dividing asunder of soul and spirit."

While the distinction between the soul and spirit is so finely drawn that only the Word of God can correctly divide them, it seems that the soul is more closely allied with the body than is the spirit. It may be that the soul is the point of communication between the spirit and the body. Sometimes the Scripture seems to use the words *soul* and *spirit* interchangeably; at other times only one will fit the context.

Simply put, when the word *soul* is used in a way that distinguishes it from *spirit,* it appears to describe the mind, will, and emotions.

The mind is part of the soulish nature, and Christians must not underestimate its function in enabling them to live overcoming, abundant lives. Repeatedly the New Testament stresses the importance of the mind. (See, for example, Romans 12:2 and Philippians 2:5.)

When a person is born again, his spirit is reborn (John 3:6). He still lives in the same body, and he still retains the same soul. His mind, will, and emotions are immediately affected by the reborn spirit, but following the new birth, he still needs to be progressively transformed by the renewing of his mind (Romans 12:2). He must learn to think differently. He must develop the mind of Christ.

To this end, the Apostle Paul gave eight characteristics of the Christian mind:

Finally, brethren, whatsoever things are true, whatsoever things are honest, whatsoever things are just, whatsoever things are pure, whatsoever things are lovely, whatsoever things are of good report; if there be any virtue, and if there be any praise, think on these things (Philippians 4:8).

We should examine every thought that comes into the mind by these eight guidelines. If it fails at any point, we should reject that thought.

It is impossible to prevent thoughts from presenting themselves to the mind. Satan is a master at introducing wrong thoughts. But while it is impossible to prevent thoughts from occurring, it is possible to control meditations. A person is not condemned because of temptations or evil thoughts that come to him, but he is responsible if he allows an evil thought to dwell in his mind and become a meditation.

A meditation is a thought that is accepted, welcomed, and entertained. David prayed, "Let the words of my mouth, and the meditation of my heart, be acceptable in thy sight, O LORD, my strength, and my redeemer" (Psalm 19:14).

When every thought is made to pass through the eight gates of Philippians 4:8 before being allowed into the room of meditation, the mind will be well on its way to renewal.

Thinking True Thoughts

Before a person permits a thought to lodge in the mind and become a meditation, he must examine it to see if it is true. The mind should not dwell on a thought if there is any question as to its authenticity. This includes reports about other people, rumors about economic trends, and news concerning government officials. We must not assume that a report is true simply because it appears in the media.

Some years ago when my family lived in St. Louis, Missouri, I read a small article in the newspaper reporting that the Vice President of the United States of America was coming to St. Louis. I was interested in seeing this high government official, so on the day he was to arrive I drove to the airport. There I inquired about the time and place of the Vice President's arrival. I learned that his airplane would take him to a small hangar away from the main terminal.

I drove to the hangar and found a parking place a few feet away from the drive that led from the main street to the hangar. Then I joined a small group of young people, members of the Vice President's political party, as they waited at the head of the drive for his entourage to pass.

The Vice President was holding a news conference in the hangar, and we waited a considerable length of time for it to conclude. At last the motorcade began moving up the drive toward us. Soon we could see the Vice President's limousine. As he reached the spot where we stood, the Vice President ordered his driver to stop. He stepped from the car and went around the entire group waiting to greet him, shaking hands with each one of us.

When he reentered his limousine and drove away, I walked the few feet to my car and turned on the radio to the city's leading news station, a member of one of the national networks. The announcer, who was on the scene to cover the Vice President's arrival and who had just participated in his news conference, reported: "The Vice President has just left the news conference. There was a small group of well-wishers waiting to greet him, but he did not stop."

To be certain of the truth, a person must have first-hand knowledge. Even then he should be cautious, for it is possible to misinterpret what he sees or hears.

A person should always be wary of a second-hand report. It is virtually impossible to relate with absolute accuracy what someone else has done or said. It is extremely difficult to recall the exact words used, and words are heavily weighted with meaning. Even if it is possible to recall the precise words used, it is difficult to retain and convey the vocal intonations and facial expressions that colored the meaning of those words. As I Corinthians 13:5-7 indicates, those who walk in love should be quick to believe good reports and slow to receive bad reports.

God never intended for humanity to be troubled with the knowledge of evil. But the Fall in the Garden of Eden corrupted the thought processes of humans. As a result the human mind now has a tendency to believe the worst, an insatiable desire for bad news.

This truth is illustrated by the wide circulation given to preposterous and demonstrably untrue rumors. For many years, the rumor has persisted that a well-known American atheist has introduced legislation in the United States Senate to remove all religious programming from the airwaves. This rumor is supported by means of mimeographed or photocopied information purporting to give the actual number of the Senate bill. There is no truth whatsoever to this allegation; the Senate bill simply does not exist. And yet over the years, hundreds of thousands of letters of protest have been sent to the Federal Communication Commission. The FCC has had to hire additional staff just to cope with the deluge of mail. The commission has conducted intense research to try to discover the origin of this rumor. As nearly as it can determine, the first allegation was made at a revival meeting in Missouri a number of years ago. The FCC has pleaded with the Christian community to realize that the rumor is false, but the letters keep pouring in.

Some people think that even though the rumor is untrue, it is good to keep responding to it in order to let a government agency know of the opposition of the Christian community to any such action. But actually this sort of response demonstrates a lack of awareness and a gullibility on the part of Christians. It reveals that many of them are willing to believe what they hear or read without bothering to do the research necessary to validate the claims. This is a weakness, not a strength. As the boy in the fable, the Christian community would cry "wolf" so long when there is no genuine threat that its voice would not be heard in a real crisis.

Some time ago, rumors circulated that Ray Kroc, the head of McDonalds, paid tithes or gave a certain percentage of his income to the Satanist movement. As a result of that unfounded accusation, many Christians stopped buying from that company. Doubtless, almost none of those who believed this false report ever bothered to check it out for themselves. They simply relied on the bad report they heard.

More recently, reports began to circulate that Proctor and Gamble also supported the Satanist movement and that their logo was actually occult symbolism. The company has tried diligently to dissuade the Christian community from this patently false report, but some continue to accept it.

A few years ago, tapes circulated across the country of talks given by a man who claimed to be a former witch and privy to much secret information. He told of an alleged scheme to take over the world, asserting that virtually every major corporation was owned by a secretive occult organization. Many Christians swallowed these claims without question. Some pastors even played the tape in their services, causing their people to believe this incredible tale of fear and hopelessness. His allegations caused at least one local congregation to arm itself with

14

rifles and shotguns to ward off the predicted occult upris-
ing. Virtually no one who embraced the message of
negativism did any checking to see whether it was true.

The fact is that the man who travelled about with that
deadly message was disfellowshipped from his local church
because of his untruths. Much of what he claimed could
easily be proven false. Time has proven the entire story
to be a fabrication.

God hates lying. He delights in those who are truthful.
"Lying lips are abomination to the LORD: but they that
deal truly are his delight" (Proverbs 12:22). Lying is one
of the things guaranteed to send a person to the horrible
lake of fire and brimstone (Revelation 21:8; 22:15). Though
a good portion of the world's population may seem to em-
brace falsehood as a way of life, the Bible declares, "The
lip of truth shall be established for ever: but a lying tongue
is but for a moment" (Proverbs 12:19).

Perhaps Philippians 4:8 lists truth as the first characteristic of a truly Christian mind because this restric-
tion alone will eliminate many thoughts from becoming
mediations.

But a thought may be true and still not be qualified
for meditation. Seven more restrictions follow.

Thinking Honest Thoughts

The second requirement of Philippians 4:8 is to subject thoughts to honesty. The Greek word *semnos* here
means "honorable."

To judge if something is honorable, a helpful question to ask is, Is this subject or action worthy of imitation by others? If it is not something God would be pleased

15

for people to do, the thought should be rejected.

It is possible for something to be true and yet to be unworthy of meditation. Perhaps a bad report about a believer who fell into sin is clearly true. But since his fall is not honorable, it is not healthy food for thought. The person who concentrates his attention on those who have fallen away will soon find himself questioning his own relationship with God and may eventually be led to follow a bad example.

There is, of course, the scriptural admonition for those who are spiritual to restore, in a spirit of meekness, believers who have fallen (Galatians 6:1). But here the attention is on the restoration of the fallen brother, not his sin.

This second qualification for the Christian mind will prevent a person from getting involved in gossip and whispering about the less than honorable actions of others. Apparently David had an understanding of this principle, for he said, "I will set no wicked thing before mine eyes: I hate the work of them that turn aside; it shall not cleave to me. A froward heart shall depart from me: I will not know a wicked person. Whoso privily slandereth his neighbour, him will I cut off: him that hath an high look and a proud heart will not I suffer" (Psalm 101:3-5).

Not only did David recognize the importance of not being influenced by the wrong example, he saw the significance of focusing on the right example. "Mine eyes shall be upon the faithful of the land, that they may dwell with me: he that walketh in a perfect way, he shall serve me" (Psalm 101:6). He continued to describe his determination not to focus on dishonorable reports: "He that worketh deceit shall not dwell within my house: he that telleth lies shall not tarry in my sight" (Psalm 101:7).

It is possible to keep wrong thoughts from becoming meditations only by replacing them with right thoughts. It is generally impossible to blank out wrong thoughts, but it is possible to superimpose right thoughts over them.

The most powerful thoughts in existence are those recorded in the Holy Bible. God said, "Let the wicked forsake his way, and the unrighteous man his thoughts . . . For my thoughts are not your thoughts, neither are your ways my ways . . . For as the heavens are higher than the earth, so are my ways higher than your ways, and my thoughts than your thoughts" (Isaiah 55:7-9).

Christians must counteract negative human thoughts with the pure thoughts of God. For example, when a believer is tempted to fret because of a spreading false report, he should meditate on these words: "Fret not thyself because of evildoers, neither be thou envious against the workers of iniquity" (Psalm 37:1).

Thinking Just Thoughts

The Greek word translated "just" in Philippians 4:8 is *dikaios,* which refers to something proper or appropriate. The third requirement for the Christian mind, then, is to ensure that each thought is proper.

One by one, God's requirements narrow the field for an acceptable thought life. It is possible for a thought to be true and even honorable, and yet it may not be appropriate at a given point in time, perhaps because of questionable motives.

I once learned something that I was extremely eager to share with another person. It had nothing to do with

17

a bad report. It was true and honest. But before I shared it with the other person, I realized my motive for wanting to tell it was faulty.

The motive is the reason why. The Scriptures identify three root sins of pride, greed, and moral impurity, and wrong motives fall in one of these categories.

For example, a person may predict to another that a certain thing will happen. It may be a good thing, worthy of imitation. But when it comes to pass the motive for meditating on it and talking about it could be pride in his ability to make accurate predictions. This ordinarily takes the form of the statement, "See, I told you so." But pride renders the thought improper. Later, the person's motive may change and it may then be appropriate to think and talk about the event.

"Set a watch, O LORD, before my mouth," David prayed, "keep the door of my lips" (Psalm 141:3).

It is impossible to be too careful in guarding one's thoughts. Solomon taught his son the importance of guarding his heart (a biblical synonym for the mind): "Keep thy heart with all diligence; for out of it are the issues of life" (Proverbs 4:23).

Jesus taught, "But those things which proceed out of the mouth come forth from the heart; and they defile the man. For out of the heart proceed evil thoughts, murders, adulteries, fornications, thefts, false witness, blasphemies: these are the things which defile a man" (Matthew 15:18-20).

Since a person will become what he thinks, the believer must be sure each thought is not only true and honorable, but also appropriate.

18

Thinking Pure Thoughts

The path to personal purity is cleaning up the thought life. Actions are the product of thoughts. Right thoughts produce right actions; wrong thoughts produce wrong actions. The attempt to break wrong habits alone will usually fail, because the wrong battle is being fought. The real battle is in the mind.

Right thinking will result in peace (Philippians 4:9). Wrong thinking will produce anxiety, fear, worry, distress, and double-mindedness.

For a thought to be worthy of meditation, not only must it be true, it must be pure. There are many ways a thought can be contaminated.

It may be immoral. Society is so saturated with suggestive advertising that immoral thoughts have become standard mental fare for multitudes. The absence of such advertising would not erase such thought patterns; the fallen nature of man inclines itself toward them even without external prompting.

Nevertheless many printed materials, movies, songs, and other media do encourage impure thoughts, and they also reveal the acceptability of such meditations to modern man. If every person were suddenly given a penny for his thoughts, an unbelievable collection of garbage would spill out.

It may be self-centered. Not every man has the same weakness. While one may wrestle with thoughts of moral impurity, another may be consumed by proud, egotistical, self-centered thoughts. He may even be proud that he does not have another's weakness. Such was the case with the Pharisee in the parable Jesus told about the prayers of the publican and the Pharisee. Similarly, if a person finds himself thinking about how important he is, how indispensible, his thoughts are impure. They are contaminated with pride.

Hebrews 12:1 implies that a specific sin easily besets each person. He must identify that sin and put it aside.

It may be greedy. The human mind is marvelously inventive at scheming ways to get ahead, even at another's expense. When the thoughts that march through the door of a person's mind are of ways to get rather than ways to give, they too are polluted. Purity and greed are antithetical. The love of money is, after all, the root of all evil (I Timothy 6:10).

Greed is a particularly deceptive sin, because it disguises itself as godliness (I Timothy 6:5). Money and material possessions pose a great temptation.

"But they that will be rich fall into temptation and a snare, and into many foolish and hurtful lusts, which drown men in destruction and perdition" (I Timothy 6:9).

A Christian should examine every thought for purity. If a thought is immoral, self-centered, or greedy, he should reject it. Such tainted thoughts will disrupt the Christian's inner peace and tranquility. Any thought that does not measure up to God's Word is impure.

David prayed, "Create in me a clean heart, O God; and renew a right spirit within me" (Psalm 51:10). He recognized that the cleansing and renewal of his inner being was a necessary step to prepare him to teach transgressors the ways of God, which would result in the conversion of sinners (Psalm 51:13).

The Christian is to refuse impure thoughts as unlike the mind of Christ.

Thinking Lovely Thoughts

Another gateway to the Christian mind is to think lovely thoughts. The Greek word translated "lovely" is *prosphiles,* meaning "pleasant."

How can a person weed out unpleasant thoughts? If he meets the previous requirements for right thought, it will not be as difficult for him to reject unlovely thoughts. Most unpleasant thoughts will already have been rejected on the basis of being untrue, dishonorable, improper, or impure.

When we examine the context of biblical warnings against grieving the Holy Spirit, we find that this sin relates primarily to words and attitudes, both of which are the products of thoughts. Ephesians 4:29-32 instructs us in this regard.

"Let no corrupt communication proceed out of your mouth. . . ." The first word of this verse indicates that believers have control over their words. "Let" implies permission. The Christian is not to permit any corrupt words to come out of his mouth. Corrupt words are the result of corrupt thoughts, while pleasant words result from pleasant thoughts.

". . . but that which is good to the use of edifying. . . ." The word *edify* means "to build up, to strengthen." The only kind of communication that should proceed out of the mouth is something that will encourage and strengthen others.

". . . that it may minister grace unto the hearers." The textbook definition of grace is "the unmerited favor of God." While this definition is certainly valid, someone has suggested a more detailed and complete definition of

grace as "the desire and power to do the will of God."

According to this definition, grace is twofold. First, grace gives the believer the desire to do right; second, it gives him the power to fulfill that desire.

The Scriptures support this definition of grace. "By the grace of God I am what I am," said Paul, "and his grace which was bestowed upon me was not in vain; but I laboured more abundantly than they all: yet not I, but the grace of God which was with me" (I Corinthians 15:10). Philippians 2:13 states, "For it is God which worketh in you both to will and to do of his good pleasure." The twofold nature of grace is seen here: the desire (to will) and the power (to do).

The believer's words are to minister grace to the hearers. This statement implies that right words will create within the hearer the desire and power to do right. Most people have had the experience of hearing words that left them dejected and deflated. They have also heard words that left them encouraged and strengthened. As Solomon said, "Death and life are in the power of the tongue" (Proverbs 18:21).

Every word spoken by the believer should minister grace, strength, power, and help to the hearer. Words should never bring fear, strife, or division, because such things breed weakness.

"And grieve not the holy Spirit of God. . . ." The Holy Spirit is grieved by words and attitudes that proceed out of the thought life. This is true because the Holy Spirit resides in the born again person's spirit, and the human spirit is closely linked to the soul, which is the residence of the mind, will, and emotions. When a Christian welcomes corrupt thoughts into his mind, the Holy Spirit

is troubled. Clothing these thoughts with words maximizes the insult to the Spirit of peace.

"Let all bitterness, and wrath, and anger, and clamour, and evil speaking, be put away from you, with all malice." These attitudes are definitely the result of unpleasant or unlovely thoughts. Christians must reject them and replace them with lovely thoughts.

"And be ye kind one to another, tenderhearted, forgiving one another, even as God for Christ's sake hath forgiven you." Pleasant thoughts are those of kindness, tenderness, and forgiveness. They are in perfect harmony with the Holy Spirit; they flow with His nature.

Thinking about Good Reports

Christians are to refuse to meditate on bad news. This policy does not mean to deny reality. Certainly many bad things are happening to people and to nations. To deny them would be self-deception. But this requirement means that the Christian must not allow his mind to dwell on bad reports. Negativisim must never become the food digested by the mind.

Proverbs 15:30 describes the positive results of a good report: "A good report maketh the bones fat." This verse may indicate that good news promotes physical as well as mental health. If a good report is mentally and physically beneficial, then a bad report is detrimental to mental and physical health. A wise person will be just as reluctant to allow diseased thoughts to settle in his mind as he would be to eat moldy, decayed, and sour food.

The state of the mind certainly affects the body. Dr. Sissela Bock, a pharmacologist, reports that fully fifty percent of all prescriptions written by medical doctors are for placebos. Some medical doctors declare that eighty percent of the nation's hospital beds are occupied by patients whose sicknesses are psychosomatic in origin.

The hypochondriac vividly demonstrates the interaction between mind and body. The victim of hypochondria is convinced that he has some dread disease. Every ache and pain is further proof that some dire malady has taken up residence. He often believes that death is at hand. Medical doctors have found themselves unable to convince hypochondriacs, even after the most thorough examinations, that nothing is wrong with them physically. The reason is that the hypochondriac does not want to hear a good report; he wants to hear that he is sick. He will go from one physician to another until he finds one who will confirm his most horrible fears. Frequently, the fear of these imaginary diseases, and the constant focus on them, results in the onset of a real physical malady.

The same is true in the spirit world. Spiritual hypochondriacs are convinced that everything is bad, nobody can live victoriously, the bottom is about to drop out, "they don't make Christians like they used to," and failure is inevitable. These people will not listen to any good report that contradicts their preconceived notions. Not surprisingly, they are frequently spiritually and physically ill.

Instead of meditating on bad reports from the news media and others, Christians must fill their minds with the Word of God. When tempted to think on the negative news, they should use that temptation as a reminder to think only on good things.

For example, if someone remarks that inflation is rapidly eating away the value of money, that chiselers are

24

ruining the welfare system, and that taxes are going up, it would be good to meditate on the words of Christ: "But seek ye first the kingdom of God, and his righteousness; and all these things shall be added unto you" (Matthew 6:33).

If someone says, "The government is full of crooks. All politicians are shysters. Our country is falling apart," a good report to think on is, "Let every soul be subject unto the higher powers. For there is no power but of God: the powers that be are ordained of God" (Romans 13:1).

What if someone reports that another Christian has fallen from grace? An appropriate response would be to meditate on these words: "Brethren, if a man be over-taken in a fault, ye which are spiritual, restore such an one in the spirit of meekness; considering thyself, lest thou also be tempted" (Galatians 6:1).

Thinking Virtuous Thoughts

Virtue means "moral excellence or goodness." It describes the conformity of life and conduct to moral laws.

How many people practice virtuous thinking? It is anybody's guess, but certainly the percentages are not too high. From locker room jokes to the double meaning of remarks exchanged in respectable surroundings, many people contaminate their minds with thoughts that are anything but morally excellent.

It has been this way for a long time. "And GOD saw that the wickedness of man was great in the earth, and that every imagination of the thoughts of his heart was only evil continually" (Genesis 6:5).

The human mind can be amazingly productive for evil.

Every piece of perverted, lewd literature in the
marketplace was conceived in the human mind. Every
X-rated film, depicting ever more horribly twisted relationships, is a product of the human mind. Every attack
by one human being on another, resulting in maimed
bodies and permanently damaged personalities, is conceived in the human mind. It would seem impossible for
the human mind to degenerate any further, but Romans
1:30 describes those who are "inventors of evil things."

When people abandon virtuous thoughts, their minds
are filled with a sick unrest, a constant craving, a
relentless search for elusive satisfaction.

The peace of God will not abide where the eight
restrictions Philippians 4:8 are ignored. When a person
entertains thoughts lacking in virtue, he rejects the genuine Christian mind, and gradually he begins to conform
to the world.

Thinking Thoughts Worthy of Praise

The last of the eight requirements for acceptable
thoughts is a perfect summary of them all.

The word *praise* comes from the Greek word *epainos,*
which means praise in the sense of approval or applause.
The implication is of something worthy of praise or approval. Thus before a Christian commits his mind to
meditate on a certain course of action, he must have
assurance that the action would be praiseworthy.

To the Christian, only the approval of God is ultimately of any value. In discussing that physical descent alone
does not qualify a person as a true Jew, Paul stated, "But
he is a Jew . . . whose praise is not of men, but of God"

(Romans 2:29). To the Corinthians, the same writer declared, "Therefore judge nothing before the time, until the Lord come, who both will bring to light the hidden things of darkness, and will make manifest the counsels of the hearts: and then shall every man have praise of God" (I Corinthians 4:5).

Peter coupled praise with two other similar results of faithfulness: "That the trial of your faith, being much more precious than of gold that perisheth, though it be tried with fire, might be found unto praise and honour and glory at the appearing of Jesus Christ" (I Peter 1:7).

When it comes to handling finances, most people are extremely sensitive. For that reason, when Paul selected someone to care for a special financial project, he chose a brother "whose praise is in the gospel throughout all the churches" (II Corinthians 8:18). He was careful to point out that the man he was sending had been chosen by the churches themselves to participate in caring for finances (II Corinthians 8:19). They selected this brother because his actions were worthy of praise.

Each person will one day stand before God to give an account for the deeds done in the body. Is it possible during this life to be certain that He will pronounce, "Well done"?

It is possible. If a person thinks only on those thoughts God would commend, he will do only those things God approves. In the final analysis, the eight requirements for acceptable thoughts are of extreme importance. They will make all the difference, not only in this life, but also in the life to come.

Believing I Can

"But I just can't do it!"

The scene could be one of many: a little girl fumbling through her piano lesson; a lad running in circles to catch a pop fly; a student stumbling over the words of the "Gettysburg Address" to be recited from memory at a school program.

But to the negative "I just can't," a determined mother replies, *"Can't* never did do anything."

This reply expresses an important truth. Every person who has ever accomplished anything worthwhile has looked at the possibilities, not the impossibilities.

There is never a shortage of people who can explain why something will not work, why it cannot be done. The cornerstone of such protests is usually one of these clinchers: "But we've always done it this way," or "But we've never done it that way."

The Bible is an extremely positive book. God enjoys accomplishing things, and He uses many different ways to fulfill His plans. When Jesus informed His disciples that it is easier for a camel to go through the eye of a needle than for a rich man to enter into the kingdom of heaven, they were startled. They asked, "Who then can be saved?" (Matthew 19:23-25).

This question gave the Lord the opportunity to state one of the greatest truths in the Scriptures. "With men this is impossible; but with God all things are possible" (Matthew 19:26). In other words, there is nothing God cannot do.

But of what value is this truth to people in their attempt to achieve difficult goals? Christians have the power of God available to help them. "I can do all things through Christ which strengtheneth me" (Philippians 4:13).

The key words here are *through Christ.* If a person has a dream, a vision, a goal, a hope, or a plan, he can accomplish it if it will bring glory to God. If he can submit it to the lordship of Jesus Christ, Jesus will provide the strength to see it fulfilled.

Being a Finder of Good

Finding fault, if not a full time pursuit, is at least an avid avocation with many. It is very easy to find fault. Few people do everything as others do; not many see everything as others see them. In homes, in the marketplace, and even in churches, it is not uncommon to see people huddled together, whispering in conspiratorial tones, their conversation centering on all that is wrong.

Finding fault tends to focus on those things closest to a person. Others may think his home is lovely; he sees only the place where the paint is faded. Someone may compliment his appearance; he concentrates on the hole in his pocket. Friends may highly regard his church; he sees its shortcomings and supposes it to be achieving less than others.

A fault-finding attitude can be devastating to a family, a church, or an organization. It creates problems where none exist. It is the product of devilish wisdom. "But if ye have bitter envying and strife in your hearts, glory not, and lie not against the truth. This wisdom descendeth not from above, but is earthly, sensual, devilish. For where envying and strife is, there is confusion and every evil work" (James 3:14-16).

Scripture is clear: strife is never of God. It is sensual; that is, it has to do with a person's senses. It seems right to him; he thinks he is justified in his carping criticism and his disgruntled discourses.

My family once attended a great church conference. It was great not just from the standpoint of attendance, though a vast number attended, but it was exceptional due to the spirit and attitude of those attending. If there was any back-corner criticism, I did not see it or hear of it. A spirit of peace and harmony prevailed; this prepared the way for mighty preaching and the majestic move of God's Spirit.

This is as it should be. "But the wisdom that is from above is first pure, then peaceable, gentle, and easy to be intreated, full of mercy and good fruits, without partiality, and without hypocrisy" (James 3:17).

It is just as easy to be a finder of good as a finder of fault. The carnal nature tends to find fault, but when a person is born again, he has the ability to look for, find, and rejoice over the good things.

Every generation has a tendency to believe that it is unique. Depending on their outlook, people will declare, "We've never had it so good," or "It's never been this bad before." While there is a certain amount of uniqueness in the last days as specific prophecies are fulfilled, there is also a great deal of sameness. The Bible proclaims that all men of every generation are sinners. Jesus compared the last days with those of Noah and Lot, which preceded them by thousands of years. Human nature does not change, God does not change, and even Satan is using the same techniques he has practiced since the beginning of his iniquitous ways. It is possible at any time to find both the good and the bad. To a large degree, what a person finds depends upon his point of view.

Paul Harvey, in his article "The Good New Days," compared our day with one century ago: "Americans are detesting and protesting pollution while forgetting that in New York during horse-and-buggy days, so many horses dropped dead that every year some 15,000 bloated carcasses had to be hauled away. If there is smog in the air New Yorkers breathe today, in 1908 there was so much pollution from horse manure and flies and fleas that 20,000 New Yorkers died from cholera."

Harvey pointed out that in the "good old days" people had a life expectancy of less than thirty years, while today's babies can expect to live more than seventy-four years and even have an excellent chance of reaching one hundred. "We complain about noise from air and truck traffic," he continued. "Iron horseshoes on cobblestone streets made a deafening din. Headlines scream that our nation's crime rate increased another two percent last year. One hundred years ago, our per-capita crime rate was double what it is today. Drug addiction, called by other names, was more prevalent than now."

This popular newsman concluded, "Search history as you will; you will find no time and no place where there has been less social ferment, less labor strife, less disease than right here right now—and your children are taller, healthier, smarter, more handsome, more capable and more prosperous than any generation which preceded theirs."

There is no point in trying to sweep negative reality under the rug of positive thinking. But neither should a person ignore positive truth just because bad people are doing evil things. A fault-finding attitude will prevent God from doing what He could do in a person's life; finding good prepares the way for Him to work powerfully.

Solomon recognized that a man may not be what he seems to be. His speech may not accurately portray the real man; it may be deceptive. But a man is what he thinks. "As he thinketh in his heart, so is he" (Proverbs 23:7).

For this reason the Christian must make every attempt to think right. He must realize that the new birth is just the beginning of his new life; now he must be progressively transformed by the renewing of his mind.

2

Fruitfulness, Security, and Abundance

It is possible for the Christian to be certain that the following three blessings will come to pass in his life: (1) spiritual productivity and fruitfulness, (2) the assurance of never falling, and (3) entering the kingdom abundantly.

Most Christians worry at some point about their fruitfulness for Christ. They wonder, Am I really producing as He wants me to? Some worry that they may fall away from a saving relationship with God, or "backslide." And then, some plod along, faithfully attending church services and doing what is expected of them, but seemingly never enjoying the abundant life that Jesus promised (John 10:10).

An Amazing Promise

The Scripture explains how to overcome these problems and to ensure that the three blessings will come to pass:

*Add to your faith virtue; and to virtue knowledge; and
to knowledge temperance; and to temperance patience; and
to patience godliness; and to godliness brotherly kindness;
and to brotherly kindness charity. For if these things be
in you, and abound, they make you that ye shall neither
be barren nor unfruitful . . . for if ye do these things, ye
shall never fall: for so an entrance shall be ministered unto
you abundantly into the everlasting kingdom of our Lord
and Saviour Jesus Christ (II Peter 1:5-11).*

This is a divine promise. God keeps His Word, and
He cannot lie. But the promise will come to pass only if
its conditions are met.

A new automobile is usually guaranteed for a certain
number of miles. Within that time, if anything goes wrong
with the engine, it will be repaired free of charge. But
if the owner takes a sledgehammer, opens the hood, and
proceeds to destroy the engine, he has invalidated the war-
ranty. He must treat the automobile with proper mainte-
nance and care.

Similarly, the foregoing scriptural promise is condi-
tional in nature. Those who make no attempt to fulfill the
conditions have no claim on the promise. But those who
follow God's directions and rely on His guidance and
power to fulfill His requirements may be certain that God
will do His part.

Scriptural Principles

In following the teaching of Scripture it is important
to understand several basic truths:
* There is never a valid excuse for violating a scrip-

tural principle.

* Violation of a scriptural principle will always produce sorrow.

* The ultimate result of violating a scriptural principle is never positive.

Many people would like to enjoy spiritual fruitfulness, assurance of security, and the abundant life—if only they could do it their way. "I don't know what I'm doing wrong," some honestly remark. "It seems I can't accomplish anything for God. Sometimes I feel cold and far from Him, and I'm certainly not living abundantly." Their problem is that the only way to receive these desired blessings is to do so God's way.

To achieve these blessings, a Christian must carefully examine each characteristic that II Peter admonishes us to acquire: faith, virtue, knowledge, temperance, patience, godliness, brotherly kindness, and charity. If he will build these godly traits into his life in the proper order, he has a promise from God of fruitfulness, security, and abundance.

Faith

Faith is the starting point. Without this vital, necessary, basic ingredient, it is impossible to live a successful Christian life.

The good news is that God has given every Christian all he needs to begin. Every Christian has faith. Moreover, the ability to believe God and the work of salvation are the gift of God. "God hath dealt to every man the measure of faith" (Romans 12:3). "For by grace are ye saved through faith; and that not of yourselves: it is the gift of

God'' (Ephesians 2:8).

An important principle in developing a successful Christian life is to agree with God always. When His Word declares something to be true, the believer must agree with it, even if he does not understand it. Not to agree with God is, in effect, to call Him a liar.

Some people protest, "But I just don't have any faith. I wish I could have faith, but I can't." They simply disagree with God and doubt His integrity. These doubters suffer the consequences of the very thing they confess: a lack of faith.

A person must not allow feelings to govern his faith. Human senses are wonderful gifts from God to allow people to communicate with the world around them, but He did not give them to govern communication with the spirit world. Christians are to walk by faith, not by sight (one of the five senses) (II Corinthians 5:7).

Galatians 2:20 summarizes the basis of Christian living: "I am crucified with Christ: nevertheless I live; yet not I, but Christ liveth in me: and the life which I now live in the flesh I live by the faith of the Son of God, who loved me, and gave himself for me."

The Christian must certainly have faith in the Son of God. The believer's everyday life is not empowered by his own mental strength but by the Son of God. The faith that is operative in the life of the believer is much more than mere human faith; it is faith imparted by Jesus Christ Himself. He has no shortage on faith; He has perfect faith. And He gives the believer all the faith he needs to live the Christian life successfully.

Every believer should confess, "I do have faith. I have faith because God gave it to me. And because God gave it to me, it is sufficient."

Virtue

"Add to your faith virtue; and to virtue knowledge" (II Peter 1:5).

Since Scripture is inspired by the Holy Spirit, each word is of great significance, and the order of words should not be overlooked. A common mistake is to add knowledge to faith, without first adding virtue. Such an attempt is counterproductive, for knowledge without virtue is dangerous. (See I Corinthians 8:1.)

The word *virtue* means "moral excellence." Someone who has virtue will separate from everything that is not morally excellent. Failure to do so is the root of most problems in the lives of Christians.

A respected Christian leader has said, "One of the greatest causes of diminishing the potential of our lives . . . is the failure to turn from all the thoughts, words, and actions which we know grieve the Spirit of God."

Either a person separates himself from sin, or his sin will separate him from fellowship with God. Many people wonder why God does not answer their prayers, even when they exercise faith (the first step given in II Peter). The Bible assures us that "the Lord's hand is not shortened, that it cannot save; neither his ear heavy, that it cannot hear" (Isaiah 59:1). The next verse, however, explains why God sometimes refuses to hear (consider) certain prayers: "But your iniquities have separated between you and your God, and your sins have hid his face from you, that he will not hear" (Isaiah 59:2).

In addition to exercising faith, then, it is necessary to develop virtue, or to cut off everything that is displeasing to God. Though a person may not struggle with gross outward sins, such as murder, adultery, stealing, and lying, he especially needs to examine himself in the areas of thoughts, words, and attitudes.

If a person knows he is not as fruitful as he should be for God, if he sometimes feels insecure in his relationship with the Lord, or if he knows that he is not experiencing a consistently abundant life, it is apparent that at some point he is violating the progression given by II Peter. In many cases, problems develop at this second step.

Knowledge

This third element remains a major gap in the Christian development of many. The knowledge spoken of here is the knowledge of the Word of God. Many Christians have a less than adequate knowledge of the Scriptures.

Many years ago, a friend was talking with me about the Scriptures, and he mentioned a saying often quoted as the Word of God. He pointed out that the saying was not in the Bible. I was certain my friend was in error, because I was sure I had read the "verse" just prior to our conversation.

When I checked the Bible and *Strong's Exhaustive Concordance,* however, I discovered that I was wrong. Though I had often heard the so-called verses of Scripture quoted and thought I had read it, it just was not there. (The "verse" was: "Spare the rod and spoil the child.") Since that time, I have always tried to be cautious about attributing something to the Word of God if I am not absolutely certain it is there.

Reverend N. A. Urshan, speaking at the graduation of Gateway College of Evangelism in 1977, mentioned some "verses" he had heard quoted which were not really in the Bible. A respected government official told him once that a "verse" which had meant so much to him was "Cleanliness is next to godliness." Reverend Urshan had to think a long time for an appropriate way to tell the gentleman that his "favorite verse" was not in the Bible.

Another time, he said, a lady stood in a service and said she was so thankful for a verse that had been very meaningful to her through the years: "Grin and bear it."

Although these examples are humorous, it is disturbingly evident that vast numbers of Christians are woefully ignorant of what the Bible actually does say.

The Book of Proverbs teaches that (1) knowledge is more valuable than gold (8:10); (2) wise men lay up knowledge (10:14); (3) a man of knowledge is a man of few words (17:27); and (4) knowledge increases a man's strength (24:5).

One of the most startling verses of Scripture on the subject of knowledge is Hosea 4:6: "My people are destroyed for lack of knowledge: because thou hast rejected knowledge, I will also reject thee, that thou shalt be no priest to me: seeing thou hast forgotten the law of thy God, I will also forget thy children."

It is impossible to overemphasize the value of knowledge of God's Word. In fact, without such knowledge, a person is destined to be unfruitful, to be insecure, and to live below the level of an abundant life.

Christians must read the Word, memorize the Word,

meditate on the Word, and as N. A. Urshan said, quoting an elder minister, "Wallow in the Word." There is no substitute for the Word, and it is impossible to be a successful Christian without knowing the Word.

Temperance

The fourth step in achieving fruitfulness in the knowledge of the Lord Jesus Christ, security in relationship with Him, and the assurance of abundant life, is to add temperance to knowledge.

Temperance is self-control. Temperance means that a Christian will control his involvement in all areas of life.

Some things he will abstain from completely. For example, the Scriptures clearly teach us to abstain from pollutions of idols, fornication, things strangled, blood, all appearance of evil, and fleshly lusts. (See Acts 15:20, 29; I Thessalonians 4:3; 5:22; I Peter 2:11.) But while abstinence touches only a few of the crisis points of life, the Christian must practice temperance in all areas.

For some, abstinence is easier than self-control. Some things are not evil in and of themselves. Those who are strong in the faith will be able to partake of these things in a temperate manner. Others, whose faith is not so strong, may find it necessary to abstain completely. "Him that is weak in the faith receive ye, but not to doubtful disputations. For one believeth that he may eat all things: another, who is weak, eateth herbs" (Romans 14:1-2). The important point here is for neither the partaker nor the abstainer to despise the other, and for the strong to handle their liberty in a way that will not cause their weaker brothers to lose faith in Christ.

Even good things can become evil when practiced without self-control. Overindulgence in any respect displays weakness of character. Commonplace things or activities, even the basic necessities of life, can become a snare to those who are not temperate.

Food. Intemperance in the use of food is a stumbling block. Proverbs 23:21 casts the drunkard and the glutton in the same role. Jesus said the right attitude toward food is to take no thought for it (Matthew 6:25). This means that Christians should see food as a simple necessity of life, not the reason for living. They are not to give it a preeminent place in their thinking or plans.

Clothing. As compared with the world population, the citizens of North America enjoy a luxurious lifestyle. The material wealth so predominate here has encouraged many people to think of various luxuries as necessities. But the Bible limits the necessities of life to two: food and clothing (I Timothy 6:8). Just as some people practice gluttony, some indulge intemperately in clothing. This form of intemperance is evident when a person consumes a significant portion of time in thinking and worrying about apparel and when large portions of his budget go toward the purchase of clothing. A good indication that a person's attitude toward clothing is wrong is the common statement, "I don't have a thing to wear." As with food, Jesus said believers should not take thought for clothing (Matthew 6:25).

Entertainment. This is a sensitive area, and one where some find it easier to be dogmatic about abstinence than to practice temperance. Certainly Christians should avoid worldly amusements or activities with worldly environments and should not make pleasure a high priority for their time and money. Some people are of the opinion, however, that all entertainment or relaxation is "of the devil" and may forbid such things as taking a ride in a car for pleasure on Sunday afternoon or visiting a theme park. For example, a Christian once mentioned to me that when she was a child she was forbidden to attend a school picnic, which consisted of school children eating their lunch in a meadow. A person may abstain from a certain morally neutral activity if he desires, but he should not pass judgment on others who feel freedom to participate in that activity.

Jesus endorsed pleasure in moderation and entertainment when appropriate. He performed His first miracle at a wedding feast, and He told the story of the prodigal son, who was welcomed home to the accompaniment of music and dancing (John 2:1-11; Luke 15:11-32).

Christians must practice temperance in every area of life. But temperance cannot be added until virtue has joined faith and knowledge has united with virtue. Some people find the most secure course to be one of abstinence even from morally acceptable pleasures because they have not developed fully in faith, virtue, and knowledge.

Patience

When we closely examine the qualities that guarantee fruitfulness, security, and abundance, it is evident that nearly all of them are traits of inward character. The next quality is patience; it is to be added to temperance.

Our age is particularly impatient. Someone has defined a split second as the time that elapses from the moment the traffic light turns green until the fellow in the car behind blows his horn. Our "hurry up" society is a cause of the modern plague of ulcers, heart trouble, headaches, and even cancer. Dr. S. I. McMillan, in his book *None of These Diseases,* clearly demonstrates the relationship between a person's attitude and his health.

If a person does not add patience to the previously listed qualities, unfruitfulness will result. Projects will fail. Feelings of insecurity will proliferate. The abundant life will be something he wishes for but never obtains.

Patience is more than just putting up with unpleasant circumstances. The true meaning depicts a beautiful trust in and dependence on God. Certainly patience includes endurance. However, the literal meaning of the Greek word *hupomone,* from which "patience" is derived, is "an abiding under." It suggests a more complete definition of patience: responding to every situation in accordance with the Word of God; to abide under the Word; to look at all things from God's viewpoint. Someone has suggested that patience is accepting a difficult situation from God without giving Him a deadline to remove it.

Many years ago my grandfather, L. D. Segraves, who was a Pentecostal preacher, was approached by a woman who asked him to pray that God would give her patience. He placed his hand on her head and began to pray, "O Lord, please send this woman tribulation." She did not fully appreciate his prayer, but it was perfectly scriptural, for "tribulation worketh patience" (Romans 5:3).

Adverse circumstances present the opportunity for the development of patience. In times of trial a person can go to the Word of God, find the principle that matches his situation, and abide "under" the Word. In this way he can use the negative force of tribulation to work for good. (See Romans 8:28.)

The Institute in Basic Youth Conflicts offers these comments concerning suffering:

Suffering will usually come from people you would least expect.

Suffering is designed to open new sections of Scripture to us.

Suffering can be used to free us from that which would hinder us from setting our affections on things above.

Suffering is most painful when we are partly at fault.

The believer should not respond to life experiences in the same way as those who have never experienced the new birth. Christians should grow and develop the trait of abiding under the Word. Before making a decision as to how to react, they should ask, "What would Jesus do?" (See I Peter 2:21.)

Godliness

"He's a godly man." One Christian will occasionally offer this assessment of another. The Greek word translated "godliness" is *eusebia,* which means "a God-ward attitude, doing that which is well pleasing to Him."

We can learn much about the meaning of words used in the Scriptures by reading the context of the various passages in which they occur. Let us examine each passage where the word *godliness* appears in order to gain valuable insight as to its meaning.

The preceding definition of godliness uses the word *attitude,* so it is no surprise to discover that II Peter links

44

godliness with holy lifestyle: "Seeing then that all these things shall be dissolved, what manner of persons ought ye to be in all holy conversation [lifestyle] and godliness [a God-ward attitude]?" (II Peter 3:11).

Paul urged Timothy to put first things first so that he would be able to lead a quiet and peaceable life in all godliness and honesty (I Timothy 2:1-2). Here again, the Bible connects godliness with lifestyle. It follows, then, that godliness is the alternative to listening to and indulging in "profane and old wives' fables" (I Timothy 4:7). Moreover, godliness has promise of both this present life and the future (I Timothy 4:8).

The full importance of attitude as related to godliness further unfolds in I Timothy 6:3-6: "If any man teach otherwise and consent not to wholesome words, even the words of our Lord Jesus Christ, and to the doctrine which is according to godliness; he is proud, knowing nothing, but doting about questions and strifes of words, whereof cometh envy, strife, railings, evil surmisings, perverse disputings of men of corrupt minds, and destitute of the truth, supposing that gain is godliness: from such withdraw thyself. But godliness with contentment is great gain."

This passage shows that godliness has a direct, dynamic relationship to words, which spring from the heart. We should note that ungodly teachers typically equate gain with godliness. In other words, they suppose that just because everything is going their way, God approves of their teaching and conduct. The passage instructs Christians to withdraw from those who adopt these ungodly attitudes.

According to II Timothy 3:5 some people will have

"a form of godliness" but will deny the power of godliness. There is enough power in a God-ward attitude to accomplish all that God wants done. It is never necessary to resort to strife, envy, railings, evil surmisings and the like. Paul told Timothy to turn away from people who had a form but not the power of godliness.

Peter declared that God "hath given unto us all things that pertain unto life and godliness, through the knowledge of him" (II Peter 1:3). The way to become godly is to get acquainted with God Himself. A person can do so through His Word and His Spirit, in even balance.

Brotherly Kindness

The story is told of a man and wife who once had a terrible argument at home just prior to going to church. They did not resolve the issue, but during the church service, as the Spirit of the Lord began to move, the husband responded with great rejoicing. When asked later how he could so easily worship when he was in the midst of an argument with his wife, he answered, "I'm not mad at God."

God has ordained, however, that a person's relationship with Him directly influences his relationship with his fellow man and vice versa. For example, if a husband does not treat his wife properly, his prayers will be hindered (I Peter 3:7).

Jesus said the proof of discipleship is to have love one to another (John 13:35). The inspired Apostle John summed it up well when he wrote, "If a man say, I love God, and hateth his brother, he is a liar: for he that loveth not his brother whom he hath seen, how can he love God whom he hath not seen? And this commandment have we from him, That he who loveth God love his brother also" (I John 4:20-21).

From these passages we learn an important principle: no man is in proper relationship with God if he is not in proper relationship with his fellow man. In the home, this principle includes the parent-child relationship; on the job, the employee-employer relationship; in the school, the teacher-student relationship; and in the church, the brother-brother relationship.

It is no accident when people falter in their relationship with God. Much of the time, growing cold spiritually and even backsliding can be traced directly to a breakdown in human relationships. Again, I John explains, "He that saith he is in the light, and hateth his brother, is in darkness even until now. He that loveth his brother abideth in the light, and there is none occasion of stumbling in him. But he that hateth his brother is in darkness, and walketh in darkness, and knoweth not whither he goeth, because that darkness hath blinded his eyes" (I John 2:9-11). What is the darkness that blinds the eyes? It is the darkness that results from a broken relationship with a fellow man.

It should be clear, then, that it is absolutely essential for fruitfulness in God's kingdom, for security in relationship with God, and for living the abundant life, to add brotherly kindness to the previous qualities. "And to godliness brotherly kindness . . ." (II Peter 1:7).

Relationship with God and relationship with one's brother are closely related. Each Christian should ask the Spirit of God to reveal any broken relationships that need healing. Mending these relationships will make all the difference in the world in his relationship with God.

Charity

The first quality—the basis of one's relationship with God—is faith; the final quality is love (charity). Love is the ultimate. All other worthy qualities lead up to the supreme quality of love.

According to I Corinthians 13, love must be the basis of all other spiritual endeavors. This great passage reveals that all the gifts of the Spirit are worthless without love. Speaking with tongues minus love is equal to noisy brass or tinkling cymbals. Even if someone has the gift of prophecy, understands all mysteries and has all knowledge and faith, he is nothing without love. Selling all he has to give to the poor, or even suffering martyrdom, is worthless without love.

I Corinthians 13:4-7 discusses the characteristics of love. Godly love is extremely patient, humble, concerned with the needs of others, and pure minded.

Scripture compares the church to the human body. (See I Corinthians 12.) This spiritual body is made up of many members, compared to hands, feet, eyes, ears, and so forth. Ephesians 4 provides further insight on this subject and teaches that Christians should endeavor to keep the unity of the Spirit until they arrive at the unity of the faith (Ephesians 4:3, 13).

The attempt to reverse this process is common, as some insist on total unity of the faith as a prerequisite to the unity of the Spirit. Jesus, however, emphasizes the same order as Ephesians 4. "When he, the Spirit of truth, is come, he will guide you into all truth" (John 16:13).

No one has arrived at the complete totality of truth. The Spirit continues to guide believers into a more complete understanding of truth. Each Christian should be aware of more truth today than he was a year ago.

If believers are to have spiritual unity as they all walk at their own pace toward unity of the faith, what is going to hold them together until they arrive at that final point? Some people suggest that the only thing which can unite people is agreement on all the fine points of doctrine (the faith). But this is not so, for very few people agree on every single point.

According to Ephesians 4:16, the body increases by the "edifying of itself in love." The quality that binds together all the members of the body of Christ is love, which Colossians 3:14 calls "the bond of perfectness." And the way to get into the body is to be baptized into it "by one Spirit" (I Corinthians 12:13).

Jesus gave one concrete evidence of discipleship: "By this shall all men know that ye are my disciples, if ye have love one to another" (John 13:35). He had no intention of negating the importance of doctrine or teaching. But unless it is based on love, all the doctrine in the world is useless, no matter how many people agree on it.

When all is said and done, only three qualities abide: faith, hope, and love; and the greatest of these is love (I Corinthians 13:13).

Love, then, is the ultimate. It is the first aspect of the fruit of the Spirit, and out of it all the others grow (Galatians 5:22-23). It is the final, highest step toward fruitfulness, security, and abundance.

The Final Analysis

The Bible promises that if the eight qualities we have discussed are in the believer and abound (exist in abundance), they will make him to be neither barren nor unfruitful in the knowledge of the Lord Jesus Christ (II Peter 1:5-11).

Most Christians are concerned about bearing fruit. They abhor the shame of a stagnant, barren life, and they earnestly desire to produce and to be an asset to the kingdom of God. This desire sometimes prompts Christians to attempt to produce fruit by their own efforts.

Joseph Bayly's parable, *The Gospel Blimp,* illustrates the folly of such schemes. In the story, a group of Christians decided to evangelize their town by a blimp that floated over the city playing gospel music and dumping gospel tracts. As the ministry developed more and more into a complicated bureaucracy, it became increasingly less effective and more irritating to the townsfolk.

There is, however, a guaranteed procedure designed to make a Christian fruitful. It is not easy. It requires total dependence on God, denial of self, and true Christian character. It is the formula presented in this chapter: faith plus virtue plus knowledge plus temperance plus patience plus godliness plus brotherly kindness plus charity.

Are these character qualities optional? No, for a person who does not have them is blind, and cannot see afar off (II Peter 1:9). He will not understand much of the Word of God, and many events of life will puzzle him, unless he adds each of the attributes II Peter mentions.

"I want to make my calling and election sure" is a common testimony. But how can a Christian do so? He can make his calling and election sure by adding each of the eight qualities, one to the other. Doing this will make his relationship with God so sure, in fact, that he will never fall (II Peter 1:10).

God has made full provision for the supply of His children's spiritual, mental, financial, social, and physical needs. He will give that provision to all who obey His Word.

The final verse of the section, II Peter 1:11, points out that acting on the instructions of verses 5-7 will guarantee an abundant entrance into the everlasting kingdom of the Lord.

Every Christian will profit if he will develop a checklist from the eight qualities of II Peter 1:5-7 and examine it carefully and frequently to see if he is making progress toward the goal of well-rounded maturity.

3

The Whole Armor of God

The only way to stand against the attacks of the devil is to wear the whole armor of God. God has designed this armor to cover the entire body. It provides the believer with both a defensive and an offensive weapon. Each portion of the armor is a symbol of a specific spiritual quality that the Christian soldier needs.

It is foolish to attempt battle with the devil in human strength. Even Michael the archangel, when contending with the devil about the body of Moses, did not dare try to defeat the devil in his own power. Rather, he said, "The Lord rebuke thee" (Jude 9). Likewise, just before the teaching about the whole armor of God, the Bible instructs believers to "be strong in the Lord, and in the power of his might" (Ephesians 6:10).

It is a human tendency to pinpoint certain people, practices, or politics as enemies. Really, though, Christians do not war against flesh and blood. According to Ephesians 6:12, the actual enemies are:

Principalities
Powers
Rulers of the darkness of this world
Spiritual wickedness in high places
For example, many people tend to identify communists as the chief enemies. But the true enemy is not actually the communists; it is the spirit behind communism, an atheistic spirit. As long as Christians do battle with the flesh and blood only, they neglect to strike at the real enemy: the spirit of evil.

Christians cannot avoid spiritual warfare. In order to be properly prepared for it, they must study and put on spiritual armor graphically described by Ephesians 6:10-18:

Finally, my brethren, be strong in the Lord, and in the power of his might. Put on the whole armour of God, that ye may be able to stand against the wiles of the devil. For we wrestle not against flesh and blood, but against principalities, against powers, against the rulers of the darkness of this world, against spiritual wickedness in high places. Wherefore take unto you the whole armour of God, that ye may be able to withstand in the evil day, and having done all, to stand. Stand therefore, having your loins girt about with truth, and having on the breastplate of righteousness; and your feet shod with the preparation of the gospel of peace; above all, taking the shield of faith, wherewith ye shall be able to quench all the fiery darts of the wicked. And take the helmet of salvation, and the sword of the Spirit, which is the word of God: praying always with all prayer and supplication in the Spirit, and watching thereunto with all perseverance and supplication for all saints.

We should notice several important points at the outset.

1. The Ephesians had been baptized in the name of the Lord Jesus and filled with the Holy Spirit (Acts 19:1-7), but they did not thereby automatically have on the whole armor. There would be no need to tell them to put on something they were already automatically wearing and using.

2. It is no accident that the *whole* armor is mentioned. Each piece of the armor has a specific and necessary role.

3. The only way to stand against the wiles of the devil is to wear the whole armor.

4. Christian warfare is not against flesh and blood. It is not physical. Never must a Christian allow his concept of spiritual battle to degenerate to the human, fleshly level. Neighbors are not the enemies. Neither are employers, employees, government, communism, or any other human institution. Although it may seem to human senses that individuals or systems are opposed to believers, it is always the spirit behind the opposition that is the real enemy.

Girding the Loins with Truth

Each part of the armor has its specific name for a reason. Paul did not just conjure up labels; the Holy Spirit directed the identification of each part.

We can identify two reasons why Christians are to gird their loins with truth.

Truth produces the right kind of children. First, in the Scriptures the loins consistently represent reproduction (Genesis 35:11). The military girdle was not a mere sword sash but a strong belt designed to cover unprotected portions of the abdomen. Thus the girdle of truth serves to protect the church's ability to produce spiritual children.

There is a strong movement today, particularly among the youth, of proselyting people to new religions. Young people are often attracted by the "brotherhood" and "family feeling" of many of these groups, which often motivate them to turn their backs on their own mothers and fathers. The teaching of such groups is usually diametrically opposed to the Word of God, though they may give it lip service. Jesus described the results of this type of reproduction in Matthew 23:15: "Woe unto you, scribes and Pharisees, hypocrites! for ye compass sea and land to make one proselyte, and when he is made, ye make him twofold more the child of hell than yourselves."

Those who make proselytes apart from the clear teaching of the Holy Bible are, in reality, producing children of hell. In other words, their efforts are saving no one. In fact, salvation becomes even more difficult, because they convince the proselyte of something that is not true.

When believers gird their loins with truth, however, they will be able to convert people to the truth. As a result, their converts will be truly born again and will enter the kingdom of God.

Truth ties everything together. A second aspect of this part of the armor of God can be seen in the function of the girdle in the Roman army. The purpose of the girdle was to hold the different pieces of a soldier's armor securely in place. In active fighting, loose pieces of armor would be troublesome and distressing, making the soldier feel awkward and unready. The belt or girdle bound the loose pieces together, creating a healthy sense of firmness and compactness and making the soldier feel that he had everything well under control. The girdle enabled him to meet the enemy's attack with united strength and confidence.

This illustration reveals the utmost importance of knowing the truth. The girdle of truth is the first piece of armor mentioned, and it is central to the proper use of the remaining articles. Without truth, the rest of the armor is loose and ill-fitting and does not serve the purposes for which it is designed.

Some people belittle doctrine and even try to minimize it so that there will be less division in Christendom. But the Greek word translated "doctrine" simply means "teaching." There is no way the believer can be justified in ignoring the teaching of the entire Word of God, even if it produces division. In fact, Jesus plainly said that He did not come to bring peace but a sword, to divide between those who held to the truth and those who did not (Matthew 10:32-38).

Pilate asked a basic question when he said, "What is truth?" (John 18:38). At the time, Jesus did not answer him. But earlier Jesus had taught that He is the way, the truth, and the life (John 14:6).

Truth is a person—Jesus. Without contradiction, Jesus must be the central figure in a Christian's life, or else all of his efforts are worthless.

It is interesting to note that truth is also a Spirit. "The Spirit is truth" (I John 5:6). This statement sheds further light on Jesus' statement that God is a Spirit (John 4:24). Moreover, it shows the identity of Jesus as the Holy Spirit, and it explains Christ's promise to come to the disciples by sending the Holy Ghost, the Spirit of truth (John 14:16-18, 26).

Thus, Jesus and the Truth and the Spirit are one and the same. They are inseparable. Romans 8:9 says that if someone does not have the Spirit of Christ, he is none of His (Romans 8:9). And there is only one Spirit (Ephesians 4:4).

Truth is a way (II Peter 2:2). It is a definite way of living. Obviously, a person cannot live any way and still be in "the way."

Truth is also part of the fruit of the Spirit (Ephesians 5:9).

That multitudes would receive the Spirit of truth prior to knowing the full truth is evident by Jesus' words in John 16:13: "Howbeit when he, the Spirit of truth, is come, he will guide you into all truth." Many people receive the Spirit before knowing the truth fully. Yet we cannot stress too firmly that the Spirit comes to reveal truth. If an individual receives the Spirit on the basis of God's grace but neglects to obey the truth that the Spirit leads him into, he will be in danger of grieving the Holy Spirit and even losing his beautiful relationship with God.

The Bereans displayed the proper attitude toward further truth. "They received the word with all readiness of mind, and searched the scriptures daily, [to see] whether those things were so" (Acts 17:11). Neither prejudice nor past teaching must hinder the sincere believer from following the Spirit of truth into the truth that sets men free (John 8:32).

The Breastplate of Righteousness

The whole armor of God is unique equipment in that it enables the believer to fight a spiritual battle. While the various pieces of this armor carry the same names as their physical counterparts, they do something no human weaponry could ever do.

The next item mentioned in Ephesians 6:14 is the breastplate of righteousness.

Some well-meaning interpreters of the Bible have remarked, "The only part of the body not covered in the armor of God is the back. Therefore, you must never turn your back on the devil."

There is certainly no need to run from the devil. If properly submitted to God, the Christian can resist the devil with the knowledge that he will flee (James 4:7). But no part of the body is left unprotected by the armor of God. Even the back is covered.

In the Roman military, the breastplate covered the front and back of the upper part of the body. It might be described as a coat of mail. The good news, then, is that even if the enemy tries to pull a sneak attack on the believer, the breastplate of righteousness offers protection.

Protection for vital organs. The breastplate protects such vital organs of the body as the heart and lungs. Spiritually, the soul and spirit are associated with the area of the body covered by the breastplate. Jesus said that everyone who believes on Him will have rivers of living water flowing from his belly (John 7:38-39).

Clearly, the breastplate of righteousness protects the vitality of the Christian's relationship with his Lord. If there is a chink in this piece, the enemy is able to strike at the very root of his relationship with God.

True righteousness does not come about by good works. All human righteousness is as filthy rags (Isaiah 64:6). Titus 3:5 makes it clear that the love of God does not come because of any works of righteousness. Sinful man could never improve himself, change himself, clean himself up, or lift himself high enough to measure up to God's holy standards. Righteousness must come from another source.

Paul put it this way: "Not having mine own righteousness, which is of the law, but that which is through the faith of Christ, the righteousness which is of God by faith" (Philippians 3:9).

In reality, Jesus stood in the believer's place that the believer might stand in His place: "For he hath made him to be sin for us, who knew no sin; that we might be made the righteousness of God in him" (II Corinthians 5:21).

Many people have the same problem today as did most of the Jews of Paul's day. They are ignorant of God's righteousness and go about to establish their own righteousness (Romans 10:3). This is a fruitless activity because "Christ is the end of the law for righteousness to every one that believeth" (Romans 10:4). Although it is hard for some people to accept, God imputes righteousness purely on the basis of faith and not works (Romans 4:4-6).

Satan's two-pronged attack. The devil uses two basic lies to cause people to lay aside the breastplate of righteousness so that he can attack their vital spiritual organs. First, he encourages the idea that they are righteous because of something they have done. Second, he whispers, "You're unworthy. Think of all the sins you've committed.''

Both of these ideas project a false righteousness that will fail when a person becomes involved in spiritual warfare. True righteousness comes by faith as a person accepts Christ's sacrifice and applies it to his life. The Christian is not to depend on anything he has done or could do, but solely on what Christ did for him at Calvary. When the devil whispers, "You're unworthy," he can respond, "Sure, but Jesus *is* worthy, and He took my place."

The Shoes of the Gospel of Peace

The Scripture clearly identifies the gospel with peace (Isaiah 52:7; Romans 10:15; Ephesians 6:15).

When a person takes away from or adds to the gospel that has been committed to men, he preaches a false gospel (Deuteronomy 4:2; Galatians 1:6-9). Certainly readers of this book would have no interest in taking away from the gospel, but sometimes it is extremely tempting to add to it.

Some people do this with the idea of making the gospel even stronger and firmer. This was the mistake of the Pharisees, who not only claimed to obey the entire law of God, but added hundreds of their own laws.

A faculty member of Christian Life College related to me the true story of a lady who was a member of a Pentecostal church. A gentleman who was not Pentecostal visited a service. In her zeal to convert him, she said, "Now you know that Jesus said, 'He that believeth and is baptized shall be saved; but he that believeth not and is not baptized shall be damned.' " Her pastor overheard the conversation and approached her with these words,

"Sister, why did you misquote the Scripture?" She replied, "Because I didn't think it was strong enough." (See Mark 16:16.)

Jesus clearly pointed out that when human commandments are added to God's commandments, God's Word is made powerless, and worship is in vain. (See Matthew 15:3, 6, 9.) It is impossible to strengthen God's Word. No one should tamper with His Word in any way. If He will not alter His Word, humans certainly have no business doing so (Psalm 89:34).

The gospel that Christians are to shod their feet with is the gospel of peace. God has never committed to mankind a "gospel" of condemnation. Such a thing would be impossible by the very definition of the word *gospel.* The gospel is literally "good news," and condemnation is never good news. "For God sent not his Son into the world to condemn the world; but that the world through him might be saved" (John 3:17).

How then can some people think that God has called them to do something even Jesus did not do? I cannot vouch for the veracity of the following story, but it does illustrate how warped thinking can become. A certain preacher was pastor of a church in a town that did not seem to be responsive to his message. That he was preaching the wrong message became clear when he stated, "We have a church building, with the doors open and the lights on. And I'm going to condemn this community for not accepting the truth."

Jesus, quoting from Isaiah 61, revealed to the people in His home town the type of ministry He would have. Luke 4:16-19 records His statement, and it includes not one word of condemnation. His was a ministry of preaching the good news to the poor, healing, deliverance, recovering of sight, and liberty. No one could hope to improve on the quality of Jesus' ministry.

Some people have strayed so far from the spirit of Christ's ministry that they would perhaps be the first to cast a stone, rather than uttering the Christ-like words, "Neither do I condemn thee: go, and sin no more" (John 8:11). But whenever people abandon the gospel of peace, they utter words that God has never committed to them. We must always remember that God has given us only one word to preach: He "hath committed unto us the word of reconciliation" (II Corinthians 5:19). Believers are ambassadors for Christ and are to stand in His stead, saying, "Be ye reconciled to God" (II Corinthians 5:20).

Regardless of the seeming success of a preacher of condemnation and the guilt he would heap upon those whose sins are covered by the blood of Jesus, his message will produce no eternal benefits. When someone declares any words other than the gospel of peace, he is not declaring the Word of God. Instead, he is usurping the divinely appointed role of the Holy Spirit (John 16:7-11).

Christians are to declare the whole counsel of God, including the reality of punishment for the disobedient. But they should never try to induce guilt in hearers by going beyond the clear Word of God into areas of personal preference.

The Shield of Faith

Christians are to take the shield above all (Ephesians 6:16). This statement does not mean that the shield of faith is more important than the other pieces of armor. The word *above* is translated from the Greek preposition *epi,* which carries the implication of superimposition. In other words, Christians are to superimpose the shield of faith over all the other pieces of armor. It works in cooperation with every other part of the armor.

In the whole armor of God, there are only two weapons: the shield and the sword. The defensive weapon is the shield of faith.

The shield is moveable and must be lifted up above all other pieces of armor, which illustrates that the role of faith is to protect the rest of the armor. Should the enemy attack the loins by introducing doubts about the truth, the believer must quickly move the shield of faith to protect himself there. If the devil attempts to pierce the breastplate of righteousness, the Christian positions the shield of faith to ward off his fiery darts.

The wording of Scripture shows that the shield of faith is sufficient to quench all the fiery darts of the wicked one. The devil can do absolutely nothing to penetrate the shield of faith if Christians will use it properly.

If a person does not use the shield of faith, he will be open prey to the devil. He will have no defense. For this reason it is absolutely essential to have faith. Without it a person cannot please God. "But without faith it is impossible to please him: for he that cometh to God must believe that he is, and that he is a rewarder of them that diligently seek him" (Hebrews 11:6).

According to this verse, faith has two necessary components: (1) belief that God is and (2) belief that God answers the prayer of a diligent seeker. Faith is not complete without both of these elements. Many people say they believe in God but are not sure whether He will hear and answer them when they pray. Any attempt to use the shield of faith under such an attitude of doubt will be a failure. The believer must be convinced that when he prays in faith, God will respond.

What is faith? Faith is "the substance of things hoped for, the evidence of things not seen" (Hebrews 11:1). Faith is substance and evidence. It is not an intangible, vague nothing. Faith is something definite. When a person has faith, that faith itself is proof positive that the thing for which he hopes will come to pass; it is the solid evidence that things which are not yet seen will come into view.

Faith is the opposite of walking by sense knowledge (seeing, hearing, feeling, tasting, and smelling). "For we walk by faith, not by sight" (II Corinthians 5:7). Faith is walking by Word knowledge asking, "What does God say?"

When Satan flings a fiery dart, the believer should not ask, "How do I feel about this" or "How does this look?" He should ask, "What does the Word say?" Then, he should speak the Word, in faith, and the fiery dart will be quenched.

The Helmet of Salvation

No part of the body is unnecessary or vestigial. As I Corinthians 12 states, the members of the body that seem to be more feeble are, in fact, necessary (verse 22), and the parts of the body that are less honorable are the parts that receive the most honor (verse 23). For example, with respect to the physical body, people tend to place extreme importance on the face. This part of the body determines, by and large, whether an individual is attractive or homely. And yet, as far as the functioning of the body is concerned, the appearance of the face is not important at all. By contrast, the brain is of utmost importance, yet it is not attractive or honored visibly.

In teaching on the whole armor of God, Paul said believers should "take the helmet of salvation" (Ephesians 6:17). To attempt to do battle with the devil in an unsaved state is as foolish as entering into combat bareheaded. The first severe blow to the head will be fatal, regardless of how well the soldier is protected elsewhere.

The first area Satan attacks is the head—the mind. He quickly gains control of the unprotected person, turning him into a virtual robot who moves, acts, speaks, and even thinks at the direction of the devil. But the person who is thus captive of Satan feels sure that he is "doing his own thing."

Christians are engaged in warfare. It never ceases. Thus it is of extreme importance that they never discard any piece of armor, even for a moment.

Once the believer has received the helmet of salvation, he must never waver in his confession. Both the heart (mind) and the mouth play vital roles in the matter of salvation. It is continually necessary to believe with the heart and confess with the mouth (Romans 10:10).

Satan's strategy against believers is to attempt to make them doubt their salvation. If he can convince a person to doubt that he is saved, he causes his victim, in effect, to remove his helmet. Then he will afflict the mind with all manner of thoughts contrary to the Word of God.

If a person has been born again according to John 3:5 and Acts 2:38, he should never confess doubt as to whether he has been saved. Such doubt is tantamount to suggesting that God does not keep His Word and does indeed turn away some who come to Him. Salvation does not depend on how a person feels, but on what God says.

If it were possible to have on every piece of armor except the helmet, all the other parts would be useless. The enemy would strike at the head. The Christian must protect his mind at all times. First of all, a person must receive salvation. Second, he must continually confess salvation and live an obedient life consistent with that confession.

The Sword of the Spirit

The only offensive weapon mentioned in connection with the whole armor of God is the sword: "the sword of the Spirit, which is the word of God" (Ephesians 6:17).

The sword Christian's have is the Word of God. The Holy Spirit uses the Word as a sword in spiritual warfare.

All true Christians have the Spirit, but some of them do not allow the Spirit to use the proper weapon. The Scriptures identify no weapon of the Spirit except the Word. The believer will be constantly on the defensive, attempting to ward off attack after attack, if his sword is dull (through lack of consistent study of the Word) or missing (through ignorance of the Word). (See Hosea 4:6.)

Some sincere people try to do battle with the devil with other weapons, but they always end up defeated. For example, some try to fight him in their own power. They assume that they are a match for the devil in their own right. They think they can just grit their teeth, slug it out toe-to-toe, and give Satan a couple of black eyes, and everything will be all right. But those who try this approach know that it does not work. If humans were a match for Satan, there would have been no need for Jesus to come to destroy the devil's works.

Some people boast of what they are going to do to the devil and ridicule him by such terms as "split-hoof." But this approach accomplishes nothing. The devil never appears dressed in a red suit, complete with pitchfork, pointed goatee, and horns. He is an angel, a fallen angel, but one who is able to transform himself into an angel of light (II Corinthians 11:14).

Jesus Christ gave the perfect example of how to battle the devil with the sword of the Spirit, the Word of God. (See Matthew 4:1-11.) Satan suggested that Jesus turn stones into bread. Jesus responded, "It is written . . ." and proceeded to quote the Word of God. Then the devil pretended to use Scripture himself. But Jesus knew he was misapplying and misquoting a passage from Psalm 91, so He said, "It is written again. . . ." Finally, Satan invited Jesus to fall down and worship him. Jesus declared, "Get thee hence, Satan: for it is written. . . ."

Three times Jesus was tempted, and three times He responded with the written Word of God. Can Christians today find any weapon superior to what He used?

People should never respond to the devil with their own words. For instance, let us suppose that the devil tempts a man to lie. He should not answer, "Leave me alone, Satan. I don't want to lie." That response may be true, but it does not have the power of the Word of God, and it will not repel Satan. Instead, he should answer, "It is written, 'All liars, shall have their part in the lake which burneth with fire and brimstone'" (Revelation 21:8). It is important to find a passage of Scripture that deals with the area of temptation and to use the Scripture against the tempter.

Jude 9 relates the interesting and instructive account of the contention between Michael the archangel and the devil over the body of Moses. Even Michael did not dare bring against the devil a "railing accusation." Instead, he said, "The Lord rebuke thee." There is no need to threaten the devil with blacking his eyes, pulling out his horns, or stomping him into the ground. Those words do not scare him at all. But he is frightened of the Word of God. Born-again believers should allow the Holy Spirit in them to use the powerful sword of the Spirit in spiritual battle.

Praying in the Spirit

The final admonition of Ephesians 6:10-18 is vital, for it is the hinge, or the pivot, upon which all of the armor of God operates. The final element is prayer: "Praying always with all prayer and supplication in the Spirit, and watching thereunto with all perseverance and supplication for all saints" (Ephesians 6:18).

The key to this verse is the phrase "in the Spirit." Much prayer is not offered in the Spirit. It is essentially carnal prayer, motivated by human reasoning and desires. There is probably no area where it is more needful to think as God does than in the area of prayer.

The Bible has much to say on the subject of praying in the Spirit. "Likewise the Spirit also helpeth our infirmities: for we know not what we should pray for as we ought: but the Spirit itself maketh intercession for us with groanings which cannot be uttered. And he that searcheth the hearts knoweth what is the mind of the Spirit, because he maketh intercession for the saints according to the will of God" (Romans 8:26-27). These two verses teach that people do not know what to pray for, so the Spirit makes intercession with unutterable groanings. When people are led of the Spirit in prayer, they always pray according to the will of God.

Praying in the Spirit builds up faith. "But ye, beloved, building up yourselves on your most holy faith, praying in the Holy Ghost" (Jude 20).

In his discussion of the proper use of the gifts of the Spirit, Paul said, "For if I pray in an unknown tongue, my spirit prayeth, but my understanding is unfruitful. What is it then? I will pray with the spirit, and I will pray with the understanding also: I will sing with the spirit, and I will sing with the understanding also" (I Corinthians 14:14-15). Earlier he said, "For he that speaketh in an unknown tongue speaketh not unto men, but unto God: for no man understandeth him; howbeit in the spirit he speaketh mysteries" (I Corinthians 14:2). Praying in the Spirit, then, often includes speaking in tongues.

In using the whole armor of God effectively, the pivotal point is to pray in the Spirit. Every Spirit-filled believer should realize that the Spirit is not given for a one-time experience but for a daily guide in powerful prayer.

4

"Study to Show Thyself Approved"

Two women, Mary and Martha, serve as perfect examples of how two types of people react to the presence of Jesus. When He came to visit Martha's home, she busied herself with those things women do when esteemed company is present. It requires no stretch of the imagination to see her scurrying from room to room, offering refreshments, pouring water, and preparing a meal. No one would have accused her of laziness. Martha was getting things done.

Meanwhile, Martha's sister, Mary, sat at the feet of Jesus and listened to His words.

Martha was "cumbered about much serving" and said, "Lord, dost thou not care that my sister hath left me to serve alone? bid her therefore that she help me" (Luke 10:40).

Jesus answered, "Martha, Martha, thou art careful and troubled about many things: but one thing is needful: and Mary hath chosen that good part, which shall not be taken away from her" (Luke 10:41-42).

Many well-meaning Christians, after the pattern of Martha, respond to the presence of Jesus with frantic efforts to "make Him feel at home" or to "do something to help the kingdom of God."

In contrast to all of Martha's breathless preparations, Mary sat at Jesus' feet and heard His word. This, Jesus said, is the only thing necessary. All of Martha's endeavors were nonessential.

"But someone's got to cook the food, or we won't have anything to eat!" It is almost possible to hear the protesting response from those of Martha's nature.

But this same Jesus is the one who turned water into wine and multiplied a few loaves and fishes into a banquet for thousands. Surely He would have been as willing to perform such a miracle in the home of close friends as for the multitude of followers on the mountain side— if it were needed. Could it be that some people fail to see God move in miraculous provision of needs because they hardly give Him an opportunity to do so?

The statement of Jesus indicates that only one thing is necessary in the world: listening to (and thereby obeying) the Word of God. The Word is the source of faith (Romans 10:17). If the believer will put aside his own fleshly attempts to "serve" God and instead listen to His Word, sufficient faith will arise in his heart to put the Word of God into action. The result of doing so will demonstrate how unnecessary and pointless all other efforts are.

Approved of God?

Every sincere Christian has spent some time pondering his place in God's kingdom. It is good to hunger to fulfill God's plan, because believers are members of His body, each with a specific function and role. Some things are common responsibilities, however. In these basic areas all should participate, at least to some degree.

While the apostles recognized that they in particular should give themselves to prayer and the ministry of the Word, each Christian has a responsibility to spend quality time in these areas. He must do so because through prayer and the Word he finds direction and receives strength. God has revealed His will in His Word. Man cannot live by bread alone, but by every Word God has spoken. Prayer and the Word renew the minds. As human thought processes are saturated with God's thoughts, faulty human viewpoints are purged and replaced with God's perfect perspective.

Christians must study the Word in order to fulfill the Great Commission. "Go ye therefore, and teach all nations . . . teaching them to observe all things whatsoever I have commanded you. . . ." (Matthew 28:19-20). If Christians cannot offer the Word to the nations, they have nothing to offer them. Believers owe it to the lost to become Word-minded, so that they may present the Bread of Life. As Paul admonished Timothy:

Study to shew thyself approved unto God, a workman that needeth not to be ashamed, rightly dividing the word of truth (II Timothy 2:15).

Christians must handle the Word properly in order to receive the approval of God. He is the sole judge as to the use of His Word.

Time and again, Christians are ashamed because they do not know the Word's answer for someone's question. Peter addressed this problem: "But sanctify the Lord God in your hearts: and be ready always to give an answer to every man that asketh you a reason of the hope that is in you with meekness and fear" (I Peter 3:15).

Each person is responsible to study the Word and to share the Word with others. "And the things that thou hast heard of me among many witnesses, the same commit thou to faithful men, who shall be able to teach others also" (II Timothy 2:2).

But how much time does the "average" Christian honestly spend in Word study?

God is helping His people to overcome their lack of diligence in studying the Word. He is putting a hunger in the hearts of His people for the Word. Pious platitudes, empty stories and surface skimming no longer satisfy the earnest student of the Word. As a result, several often neglected principles are coming to light, and believers are understanding their importance. Let us briefly discuss some of them.

Children should be trained in a Christian atmosphere, by godly teachers, with the eternal Word of God as the foundation. (See Psalm 26:4-5; Proverbs 19:27; 22:6.) Many children who lacked godly training at home or school have grown into adults and are attempting to live for God without the solid foundation of the Word. To overcome this problem, today thousands of thoughtful Christian parents are enrolling their children in Christian schools

74

or teaching them at home, because they realize that the future of their children and of the nation rests on decisive action in this area.

Churches must prayerfully consider whether they are placing appropriate emphasis on the ministry of the Word. It is possible to depart from the biblical pattern gradually and to be directed by the world's social mind until the church puts more emphasis on activities than on ministries.

Adults must set aside quality time, regularly, to study the Word. Many people have good intentions, but unless they give a definite priority to Bible study, they will never fulfill those intentions. They must have a definite time, a definite program, a definite course of study. Bible study time must be quality time that they will not allow anything to interrupt.

A More Sure Word

If God were to speak in an audible voice, some people would perhaps be more willing to believe Him and to act on His Word. If His Word thundered from the heavens, perhaps they would no longer doubt His ability to perform His promises.

There have been times when just such audible manifestations of God's voice have occurred. He spoke in such a way to Noah, Moses, Samuel, Elijah, and many others. Were these verbal revelations of God's will His supreme plan of communication? Or does He have a method even greater?

II Peter 1:16-21 provides an answer: "For we have not followed cunningly devised fables, when we made known unto you the power and coming of our Lord Jesus Christ, but were eyewitnesses of his majesty. For he received from God the Father honour and glory, when there came such a voice to him from the excellent glory, This is my beloved Son, in whom I am well pleased. And this voice which came from heaven we heard, when we were with him in the holy mount. We have also a more sure word of prophecy; whereunto ye do well that ye take heed, as unto a light that shineth in a dark place, until the day dawn, and the day star arise in your hearts: knowing this first, that no prophecy of the Scripture is of any private interpretation. For the prophecy came not in old time by the will of man: but holy men of God spake as they were moved by the Holy Ghost."

Christians are not followers of cunningly devised fables, but they have two initial proofs of Christ's deity: (1) the early Christians were eyewitnesses of His majesty, and (2) they heard an audible voice from heaven saying, "This is my beloved Son, in whom I am well pleased." At the outset, then, Peter's claim for the validity of Christ's ministry is twofold: they saw something and heard something. In other words, they perceived the witness with their physical senses.

Today some declare, "Oh, if only God would speak to me in a voice I could hear with my ears!" or "If only an angel would appear to me!" Such an attitude suggests that there is no greater revelation than what the senses can monitor and that all doubts could be erased by such a spectacular event. But is seeing with the eyes and hearing with the ears God's highest form of revelation? Or does He have a higher way, a superior mode of making Himself known to man?

Indeed He does, for after the previous claims, the inspired Apostle Peter continued, "We have also a more sure word of prophecy." In other words, the revelation we have is a more sure Word than what the eyes and ears can perceive. Consequently, we should take heed to this Word, which is like a light shining in a dark place.

What is this superior revelation? It is the Scripture, which came through holy men of God as they were moved by the Holy Ghost. The written Word of God, miraculously inspired and preserved by God Himself, is more certain, more sure, more definite, and more specific than anything someone can see, hear, or otherwise experience with the human senses.

This is true because "no prophecy of the scripture is of any private interpretation." The Scripture did not originate with man; God inspired it. No one can quibble over what the Scripture actually states, though people may disagree over its meaning. On the other hand, visions and audible voices are of private interpretation.

When an audible voice spoke from heaven during Jesus' ministry, some reported that it was thunder and others identified it as an angel (John 12:29). Almost invariably, two men who see the same event will give different reports of what actually transpired. The written Word is superior because everyone can easily see what it says.

This is not to say that angels do not appear today or that God never speaks in an audible voice. Indeed, God sometimes uses these methods. But revelations to the human senses are valid only as long as they measure up to the written Word of God. The moment they vary in any degree, they are to be spurned as false and deceptive. The reason why we must test all supernatural experiences by the Word of God is because "Satan himself is transformed into an angel of light" (II Corinthians 11:14). If angelic voices and appearances were superior to the written Word, there would be no end of the havoc Satan would cause. As it is, numerous cults have originated with voices heard or spirit beings seen by their founders.

Jesus said to Thomas, who said, "I'll believe only if I see," "Thomas, because thou hast seen me, thou hast believed: blessed are they that have not seen, and yet have believed" (John 20:29). Clearly, the superior faith is not that which insists on appeals to the physical senses, but that which believes regardless. It is the faith that accepts the Scriptures as the inspired, infallible, inerrant Word of God without requiring angelic visitations or voices from heaven.

Some people may say, "If I heard God speak, I would believe and obey without question." But the written Word is more definite and sure than an audible word. A person can stand more firmly upon the written Word of God than upon audible voices or visible appearances. Those who step out by faith on the Bible's promises can know that God will work all things together for their good. There is no need to question any portion of the Scripture. It is God's Word, and it cannot fail.

It is regrettable that so many know so little about the Word that God has so carefully preserved for them. More than ever, this is the day to stop looking for signs and circumstances and to begin looking into the Holy Bible, the more sure Word.

Reactions to the Word

When people are confronted with the Word of God, they respond in one of two ways. Either they receive the Word, believe it, and act on it, or they reject the Word. The latter reaction can be exhibited in a variety of ways. Some people simply walk out of the church; others call the Word into question, doubting its authenticity with varying degrees of sophistication.

These two reactions are evident in the lives of two of Judah's kings, father and son. The father was Josiah and the son Eliakim, or Jehoiakim as he was renamed by the king of Egypt. Josiah, one of the rare good kings during this period, was eight years old when he began to reign in Judah. His heart was tender toward the things of God, and he was obedient to the Lord to the full extent of his knowledge.

One day, Josiah received word that Hilkiah, the high priest, had discovered "the book of the law in the house of the LORD" (II Kings 22:8). When Shaphan, the scribe, read the words of the book to the king, King Josiah rent his clothes (verse 11). His first reaction to the Word was not defensiveness or an attempt to belittle the Word, but repentance. Right away, Josiah launched an all-out campaign to operate his kingdom according to the Word of God.

He read the Word of God to all the people of Judah (II Kings 23:2). He made a covenant with God to obey the book (verse 3). He purged the temple (verse 4). He removed from the priesthood those engaged in idolatry (verse 5). He destroyed the images (verse 6). He stripped the sodomites of their special privileges (verse 7). He removed the high places Solomon had introduced and broke down the altar Jeroboam had built at Bethel (verses 13-15). In short, Josiah cleaned up Judah from theological liberalism, immorality, idolatry, and the occult. Then Judah kept a passover that surpassed all those observed since the days of the judges.

Josiah's repentance was so complete that the Bible says, "And like unto him was there no king before him, that turned to the LORD with all his heart, and with all his soul, and with all his might, according to all the law of Moses; neither after him arose there any like him" (II Kings 23:25).

Josiah's reaction to hearing the Word of God should be an example to every sincere Christian. But, sadly, many mimic the response of Josiah's son, Jehoiakim.

In the fourth year of Jehoiakim's reign over Judah, God spoke to the prophet Jeremiah with a word of judgment against Israel, Judah, and all the nations. It was God's desire that Judah would, when they heard of the evil coming to them, repent (Jeremiah 36:3).

After Baruch, Jeremiah's scribe, had written God's words on a scroll, he read it at the temple. When Michaiah the son of the scribe Shaphan heard it, he related the message to the princes, who demanded that Baruch come and read the words to them. After the princes heard the words, inquired as to the method of their transmission, and warned Baruch to go into hiding with Jeremiah, they retained the roll in the scribe Elishama's quarters and went to tell the king about its contents. Jehoiakim sent Jehudi to get the roll. Then Jehudi read it to the king. What was the king's reaction?

"And it came to pass, that when Jehudi had read three

or four leaves, he cut it with the penknife and cast it into the fire that was on the hearth, until all the roll was consumed in the fire that was on the hearth. Yet they were not afraid, nor rent their garments, neither the king, nor any of his servants that heard all these words" (Jeremiah 36:23-24).

Thus the response of Jehoiakim to hearing God's Word was just the opposite that of his father, Josiah. Josiah repented and acted on the Word; Jehoiakim showed his contempt by burning it and ignoring its warnings. But Jehoiakim's destruction of the scroll on which the Word was written did not destroy the Word itself. The words were resident within God Himself, and He commanded Jeremiah to write them again. Not one word was lost.

People today still follow the example of these two kings. First, some people, when they hear or read the Word, are convicted and respond with repentance and a change in behavior. It is a special joy to minister to that kind of person. He is always the first one in the altar. He does not hesitate to sacrifice personally or change his lifestyle drastically, if he sees that the Word of God requires it. He leaves no stone unturned in his effort to please God. He places top priority on obedience to God and gives God everything he has. He is like Josiah, who destroyed images and orchestrated a passover unlike any since the judges.

On the other hand, many people react to the Word as did Jehoiakim. First, they deny its application to them. This occurs very simply, without a word being spoken, when an individual refuses to respond in repentance. In other words, a man does not have to say, "This has no application to me." He does not have to say this with his mouth; he says it with his actions. This kind of person refuses to change his lifestyle or to do anything that calls for personal sacrifice. He sees no reason to change the way he is living. He may excuse himself by saying, "Well, that's just this preacher's opinion. Others see it different-ly." As a result, he never responds to any preaching. He does what seems right in his own eyes.

A similar and more subtle reaction happens when people call the Word of God into question and therefore do not apply it to their lives. They may say, "We are not absolutely sure what the original reading was concerning this teaching. Textual critics differ in their opinions." As a result they do not heed or obey the Word of God either.

A man who wants to be blessed of God will, as Josiah, respond to God's Word in repentance and reformation. The casual reaction of Jehoiakim brings not a blessing, but a curse: "And I will punish him and his seed and his servants for their iniquity" (Jeremiah 36:31).

5

The Church as a Family

The family is the original institution established by God upon the earth. It precedes even the church. The Old Testament is primarily a record of God's dealing with families. The Bible is exact in recording genealogies and shows precisely the family lines through which Jesus came.

The human family serves as a prototype for the family of God as revealed in the church. The words of Jesus in Mark 10:29-30 provide an indication of this truth:

There is no man that hath left house, or brethren, or sisters, or father, or mother, or wife, or children, or lands, for my sake, and the gospel's, but he shall receive an hundredfold now in this time, houses, and brethren, and sisters, and mothers, and children, and lands, with persecutions; and in the world to come eternal life.

The following observation in no way minimizes God's

promise of an abundant blessing on financial giving. Many verses of Scripture teach the value of giving and promise generous returns. But those who use Mark 10:30 to teach that God promises a hundredfold return on money or houses are taking it out of context. They claim that if a person gives one house to God he will receive one hundred houses or one house worth one hundred times as much during his lifetime on this earth.

The emphasis here is not on houses, however, but on family relationships. No one suggests that if a man loses one wife for the gospel's sake he will receive one hundred wives, or that if he forsakes one mother, he will receive one hundred mothers. Rather, this passage reveals a truth about family relationships within the body of Christ. Whatever a person must forsake in this regard, he will receive abundant repayment for in God's family. No longer is a believer limited to a physical brother or two; suddenly he has literally thousands of brothers, sisters, mothers, fathers, and houses.

The body of Christ is intended to work as a family— a family operating under God's order. On one occasion, when Jesus' mother and brothers came to see Him, He asked, "Who is my mother? and who are my brethren?" Then He stretched out His hand toward His disciples and said, "Behold my mother and my brethren! For whosoever shall do the will of my Father which is in heaven, the same is my brother, and sister, and mother" (Matthew 12:48-50).

The Bible emphasizes this type of relationship immediately following the outpouring of the Holy Spirit on the Day of Pentecost.

The believers continued steadfastly in fellowship (Acts 2:42).

Daily, they broke bread from house to house (Acts 2:46).

They did not retain ownership of goods but considered them common property (Acts 2:44-45; 4:32).

They taught daily in every house (Acts 5:42).

There was a daily ministration of food (6:1-2).

Some people who are unable to grasp the significance of the unity of the Early Church protest that the believers were out of God's will in this family relationship, particularly in selling their property and establishing a common treasury. But had the early Christians not done so, they would have lost all of their personal possessions anyway in the destruction of Jerusalem in A.D. 70.

This example does not mean that God wills for each generation of believers to sell all their possessions and live in a communal fashion. The New Testament supports the principle of private ownership and teaches the need for diligent work to support one's family. The Epistles do not indicate that churches in other areas followed the practice of common ownership. This early practice does show, however, that the divine design of the Christian community is a family, a perfect vehicle through which to express God's love one to another.

Covenant Life

When we examine the Early Church for distinctives that either brought about, or were a result of, the believers' unique position of power and influence, one of the most outstanding characteristics is their mutual covenant and lack of selfishness.

While the concept of common property is a bit

frightening to the capitalistic mind, we can learn much from the example of those devout Christians. North Americans are certainly in no danger of being too close to the verge of "spiritual communism." On the contrary, self-centeredness, selfishness, and self-sufficiency are all too prevalent. Rather than being on the brink of radicalism in the direction of communal living, they are at the opposite extreme of self-determination, suspiciously like the ancient Israelites who each "did that which was right in his own eyes" (Judges 21:25).

In early America, the Pilgrims and Puritans firmly believed that they were called of God to establish a Christian society. Thus their first order of business in developing a society in the New World was to establish churches around which their villages were formed. Out of necessity, these early settlers made firm covenants together— they would stand or fall together. Many years later, when the Founding Fathers met to consider a declaration of independence from Great Britain, Benjamin Franklin reportedly remarked, "Gentlemen, we must all hang together, or we will certainly hang separately."

Inherent in pioneering the New World was the knowledge of the importance of unity, oneness, and common purpose. The church desperately needs these traits today. A commitment to a local body, a willingness to submit, a concern for one's brothers and sisters that demonstrates itself in action—these qualities are often lacking when we compare today's church to that of the New Testament.

While believers call one another "brother" and "sister," they must go beyond this formality and really begin to think of those God has placed them with as members of their family. A good scriptural basis upon which to begin practicing this new awareness is Galatians 6:10: "As we have therefore opportunity, let us do good unto all men, especially unto them who are of the household of faith."

The family of God is an extended family. It must not be limited to a localized area or identified along racial or ethnic lines. It is literally a universal family as Paul recognized, declaring, "For this cause I bow my knees unto the Father of our Lord Jesus Christ, of whom the whole family in heaven and earth is named" (Ephesians 3:14-15).

6

As White as Snow

One day I looked out my office window to see a fresh blanket of snow. The flakes danced merrily about as they continued to fall. Children tossed snowballs and rolled in the deep snowfall.

Freshly fallen snow is such a beautiful sight that it is standard fare for calendars and Christmas cards. An ugly, barren landscape can be completely transformed by snow, as can the back alleys, with their rutted paths and ever-present garbage cans. There is no purer white than that of new snow.

Even though the weather inconveniences us at times, I thank God for the snow. It reminds me of a truth so important, so vital, that without it I could not be saved. That truth is expressed in Isaiah 1:18:

Come now, and let us reason together, saith the LORD: though your sins be as scarlet, they shall be as white as snow; though they be red like crimson, they shall be as wool.

No matter how ugly and despicable a person's life has

been, and regardless of the scarlet brilliance of his sins, God can make him beautiful and white.

But God does not just cover up sins; He removes them. "As far as the east is from the west, so far hath he removed our transgressions from us" (Psalm 103:12). While there is a North Pole and a South Pole, it is impossible to measure the distance from the east to the west. The symbolism here is that God has taken sins so far away that no one will ever find them. Micah 7:19 puts it this way: "Thou wilt cast all their sins into the depths of the sea."

This miracle of forgiveness is accomplished through the sacrifice of Jesus Christ, who was made sin for us, "that we might be made the righteousness of God in him" (II Corinthians 5:21).

It is God's nature to forgive. He does not have to be in a certain mood to cleanse people from sin. He is always ready to remove transgressions, whenever people are ready to confess them in repentance. Writing to Christians who had already experienced initial forgiveness, John said, "If we confess our sins, he is faithful and just to forgive us our sins, and to cleanse us from all unrighteousness" (I John 1:9).

God does more than pardon sin in the human sense. A pardon remits the penalty of breaking the law, but it does not erase the record that the recipient was guilty of breaking the law. God does not just remove the penalty; He declares men innocent.

Human beings could never merit God's forgiveness. While sin has wages (death), eternal life is a gift (Romans 6:23). Nothing can be done to earn a gift. If God counted men righteous because of anything they did, eternal life would then be a just reward and not a gift (Romans 4:4). But salvation is completely by grace, not by any works of which people can boast (Ephesians 2:8-9).

God wants to reason with people, because such an arrangement as this seems unreasonable to the human mind. It seems that a person ought to do something to cleanse himself—that since he has committed the sins, he should somehow "uncommit" them. But he cannot do so. A person's only hope is to allow God to take his scarlet, crimson sins and transform them, miraculously, into the white purity of snow and wool.

Hope for the Fallen

Judas Iscariot. What mental image does his name bring to mind—traitor, thief, turncoat, hypocrite?

Most people do not think of Judas as an apostle and minister—one of the Twelve. In the Upper Room, however, Peter pointed out that Judas "was numbered with us, and had obtained part of this ministry" (Acts 1:17). Later, in the disciples' prayer for God's direction in the choice of a replacement, they said, "That he may take part of this ministry and apostleship, from which Judas by transgression fell" (Acts 1:25).

It is a fact; Judas was one of the original twelve apostles. He had actually obtained a part of the ministry and apostleship. When Jesus sent out the Twelve and gave them power against unclean spirits, the ability to heal all manner of sickness and disease, Judas was one of them (Matthew 10:1-4). Without a doubt, he participated in the miracle ministry, casting out evil spirits and healing the sick.

In retrospect, the writers of the Gospels revealed his flaws. But at the time, Judas was just "one of the boys." His story demonstrates the insidious nature of deception and the gradual nature of apostasy. Judas was not the first nor the last person to fall from grace. And no one is immune to Satan's attacks.

Much has been written in an attempt to justify Judas in his betrayal, but such psychological efforts are fruitless. His problem was simply sin. Judas knew what was right, was personally acquainted with the Master, and participated in the work of the ministry. He was just as much one of the twelve apostles as Peter or John.

What, after all, was the difference between the sin of Judas and that of Peter? Peter denied that he knew Jesus, while Judas admitted that he knew Him. Peter's denial was followed by bitter weeping, while Judas's betrayal was followed by repentance (Matthew 26:75; 27:3). Indeed, Judas confessed his sin, saying, "I have sinned in that I have betrayed the innocent blood" (Matthew 27:4).

The crucial difference is in what happened next. Judas went out and hanged himself. Much theorizing has been done on this subject. Apparently Judas could not believe that he could receive forgiveness for a sin of that magnitude, or perhaps he could not forgive himself. Peter, however, must have had some hope of pardon, for he found himself back with the remaining disciples.

Scripture teaches that "evil men and seducers shall wax worse and worse, deceiving, and being deceived" (II Timothy 3:13). What is the antidote to deception? It is to "continue thou in the things which thou hast learned and hast been assured of" (II Timothy 3:14).

While many people will err from the truth and be overtaken in a fault, the Bible gives clear guidance as to the proper reaction to them: "Ye which are spiritual, restore such an one in the spirit of meekness; considering thyself, lest thou also be tempted" (Galatians 6:1). "Convert him . . . [for] he which converteth the sinner from the error of his way shall save a soul from death, and shall hide a multitude of sins" (James 5:19).

Satan's attacks on individuals are having some measure of success today, just as they always have. But those who have fallen should realize that God loves them still and stands ready to forgive and forget. And everyone should remember the duty to restore and convert the fallen, not to condemn and ostracize.

7

Prosperity and Success

The Bible is a book of promises. Repeatedly it declares, "If you will do this, that will happen." God cannot lie (Titus 1:2). He is bound by His Word. Therefore, when a person has a certain need, he should discover how to obtain the answer, act on the scriptural principle, and rest assured that God will fulfill His part of the covenant.

One of the many promises in the Bible is that of prosperity and success. (See, for example, Joshua 1:8.) This is not prosperity and success as defined by materialism, but by God.

Psalm 1 defines the steps to certain ruin, as well as the path to scriptural success. According to this psalm, certain individuals are bound for ultimate defeat:

1. The one who acts on the counsel of the ungodly.
2. The one who stands in the way of sinners.
3. The one who sits with the scornful.

The psalm identifies only one type of person who is

bound for success: The one who delights in the Word of God, and who also meditates on that Word day and night. The person who follows the latter approach will become "like a tree planted by the rivers of water" (Psalm 1:3). In other words, he will become stable, steadfast, dependable, and healthy. A tree by a river has a constant source of life. Likewise, the person who delights in the Word and meditates on it will constantly be refreshed by the living Word.

Those who seek success and prosperity in ways contrary to Scripture have made two words famous: "If only."

"If only I had arrived a few minutes earlier (or later)."

"If only I had said this instead of that." But the person who meditates on the Word "bringeth forth his fruit in his season" (Psalm 1:3). When it is time to produce, he produces. He is never late or early and never the victim of circumstances. If he does not attain a desired goal on schedule, he rests in the knowledge that the time was not right. If something develops before he anticipated it, he knows that God has brought it about for a reason.

Many people constantly fret about being "washed up." Even many who are "prosperous" by standards foreign to the Scriptures are continually on the thin edge of despair, fearing the loss of their wealth or popularity. But the person who meditates on the Word knows that "his leaf also shall not wither" (Psalm 1:3). The leaves of any tree—even a tree planted by the rivers of water— finally wither, die, and fall off. But the point here is that the leaves will not wither out of season. When it is time for various phases of life to come to an end, they will, but not one moment before.

What a dynamic principle this is: the person who delights in and meditates on the law of the LORD will never do anything that fails to prosper.

Why do so many Christians begin projects that fail? Many projects fail because they are not born of a mind that constantly feeds on the Word. They are born of the natural thinking process only, or even more dangerously, they may be produced by a spirit of greed or selfishness. When a person renews his mind by the Word, however, it will reveal the fallacies in many plans, preventing defeat.

If those who meditate on the Word are like a well-watered, healthy tree, how does Psalm 1 picture those who do otherwise? "The ungodly . . . are like the chaff which the wind driveth away" (Psalm 1:4).

Christians need to get into the Word, memorize it, and meditate on it. These simple actions will set in motion a chain of events that bring about spiritual contentment and success exceeding their fondest expectations.

From Failure to Success

How many times did Abraham Lincoln try and fail? He was defeated in many of his efforts to attain elected office. His persistence ultimately produced victory, however, and he was elected as the sixteenth President of the United States of America.

The old saying is, "If at first you don't succeed, try, try again." Perhaps Abraham Lincoln had the philosophy of that statement burned into his consciousness as he educated himself by the flickering light of the fireplace.

The Holy Bible is replete with examples of those who

tried and failed miserably, only to come back in blazing glory. The Bible is, in large part, the account of evident defeat turned into glorious victory.

If people fail in a given endeavor, their human reasoning sometimes suggests that they should pack up and try elsewhere. They decide to get a fresh start.

For many men, Jerusalem was a city of failure. There Peter brazenly denied Jesus, and there Judas betrayed the Lord. It was there, in a moment of supreme crisis, that the disciples forsook Jesus and fled (Matthew 26:56). Perhaps they wondered if they could bear to look upon those familiar scenes again, with the certain knowledge that the very buildings, trees and stones would trigger memories of defeat. Maybe they considered leaving Jerusalem behind and making a fresh start in another city.

It is impossible to know the thoughts that coursed through the disciples' minds. But surely there was bitter regret and remorse over their weakness, especially after certain brash predictions made by men like Peter.

After Jesus' resurrection, however, He commanded them not to depart from Jerusalem (Acts 1:4). They were to stay in the city until they received a certain promise, a promise that would turn their lives from uncertainty to a positive, forceful consciousness of victory.

In the same city where Peter had denied the Lord and the disciples had forsaken Jesus and fled, the Holy Spirit fell on them all. In a moment of time, the same fisherman who had wilted before the persistent questioning of maidens stood boldly and declared the lordship of Jesus before a large audience of curious Jews. And the other disciples firmly supported Peter in his message that day. From evident defeat and apparent disintegration of their dreams, the disciples turned the corner to utter victory and the conversion of three thousand in one day.

What made the difference? They had a sure word from the Lord, and they obeyed His word until they received the promised Holy Spirit.

One certain element of success is to have a positive word from the Lord. When the Lord has spoken, a person can be certain of victory. He may not know the when or the how, but he knows the what. Jesus commanded the disciples where to wait and what to wait for. He did not tell them the when. He just instructed them to wait until (Luke 24:49).

This account reveals an important principle: if a person receives a word from God that pertains to him, then he can stand on it firmly until it comes to pass. Moreover, lest the devil should whisper that God has not spoken in his case, he should realize that God's holy Word covers virtually every aspect of human existence. He can find a word there to cover the many situations he will face.

In conjunction with the Word, the disciples received the Spirit. The Word and the Spirit form a combination against which no demon can stand and no failure can remain. The Word is the sword of the Spirit, and these two elements combine to cut through the undergrowth of failure.

After a person experiences the wonderful baptism of the Holy Spirit, the next step to total victory in a situation is to find a word from God that applies to that situation. He can then be sure of success, if he is willing to wait "until."

Goals

Every time one year closes and a new one begins, people think of new goals they would like to accomplish. A new year is simply a convenience for marking time, but it is also a good point to assess achievements during the previous twelve months and set meaningful goals for the future.

There are plenty of jokes about making New Year's resolutions, which is really a form of goal-setting. But the jesting does point to a reality: many who set goals are helpless to reach them, and many others never bother, since they are convinced the situation is hopeless. The vast majority of people go on, year in and year out, never changing, never improving, and never accomplishing, because they believe that doing so is beyond their ability. From time to time they offer lame wishes ("I really would like to lose weight," or "I'd give anything to know how to play the piano,") and then follow the wishes with lame excuses ("But I just crave sweets," or "I never could understand what all those little marks in the song books mean").

Goal-setting is a biblical practice and something without which people rarely accomplish anything.

Philippians 3:14 is a supreme example of goal-setting: "I press toward the mark for the prize of the high calling of God in Christ Jesus." This verse expresses the highest goal for which anyone could aim. The principles that propel a person toward this lofty ideal will certainly work to achieve any lesser target.

Paul's "pressing toward" was based on another action he had already taken, revealed by Philippians 3:4-13.

100

Briefly stated, in his effort to reach a high goal, Paul forgot the past.

Many people are stymied in their hopes for the future by the mistakes of the past. By constantly thinking on what has been, and using such statements as, "If only . . . ," these people allow the defeated past to ruin the spotless future.

The past that Paul forgot was a past that many would consider of great merit, something of which to be proud and on which to build. His past, which he counted as dung, consisted of previous accomplishments that had once been of great importance to him. It included his ancestry and religion. But Paul realized that these things would certainly not help him reach his new goal, so he forgot them.

One of the most valuable things a person can do is to forget his past. He must not allow his past to shackle his future. He should adopt Philippians 4:13 as his slogan to achieve his goals: "I can do all things through Christ which strengtheneth me." Whenever a person is tempted to give up, as everyone probably has been on many occasions, he should vocalize that statement of Scripture. He should make it a part of him, even as did Paul. In so doing, he will, as Paul did, certainly reach the worthy goals he has set.

The Mythical Lion

Why do some people accomplish great things in life while others just plod along, barely holding on to the status quo? There are many reasons, of course. Perhaps one of the most predominant is what we can call the "Mythical Lion Syndrome." It is seen in Proverbs 22:13:

"The slothful man saith, There is a lion without, I shall be slain in the streets."

What a perfect excuse for doing nothing! After all, who can blame a person for wanting to stay at home when a man-eating lion is prowling the streets? Any sensible person would do the same. The only problem with this excuse is that there is no lion.

The human mind is a marvelous machine. For all practical purposes, the things it imagines to be so, are so. People react as if the things they imagine are really true. In one experiment, the participants vividly imagined themselves to be in another place, such as on a sandy seashore. The researchers discovered that the human body responded to the imagined picture just as if the person were really there.

Many people refuse to attempt anything different, unusual, or "risky," because they are fearful of the "lion in the streets." They excuse their lack of effort with statements such as, "I would really like to try that, but I'm afraid . . . ," or "I wish I could do the things he is doing, but with my luck . . . ." The sad thing about these excuses is that multitudes allow nonexistent dangers to prevent them from accomplishing great things for God.

The twelve spies sent to search out the land of Canaan were not to decide whether or not it was possible to take the land. God had already decided that. They were only to search out the promises and the means of achieving them, not to pass judgment on the possibilities. Moses instructed them, "Be ye of good courage" (Numbers 13:20).

However, when they returned with their fearful report and their low self-image ("We were in our own sight as grasshoppers"), they infected the Israelites with their unbelief (Numbers 13:33). The people began to imagine mythical "lions": "And wherefore hath the LORD brought us unto this land, to fall by the sword, that our wives and our children should be a prey?" (Numbers 14:3).

God had already promised them victory, but they excused their lack of effort by an imagined defeat. Since they thought they would be defeated, they were—for all practical purposes—defeated.

The nation of Israel paid a dear price for its slothfulness. But their little ones, the very ones whom they used to excuse their lack of effort, later went in and possessed the land (Numbers 14:31).

This story teaches Christians to step out on the promises of God. They need to leave the warm security of present positions and venture out into the bright sunlight of God's higher purposes. God wants everyone to grow, to go from faith to faith and from glory to glory. "But the path of the just is as the shining light, that shineth more and more unto the perfect day" (Proverbs 4:18).

God's promises are His enablements. He never commands people to do something that He will not strengthen them to do.

One man said that his idea of hell would be to stand before God and have God tell him all the things he could have done if he had only tried. While the Bible teaches that there is a literal hell, this statement is revealing. Many people waste their full potential because they are fearful of failure.

How does a child learn to walk? By falling. Christians are not guaranteed that they will never make a mistake or fall temporarily, but they are guaranteed that they will never be utterly cast down. "The steps of a good man are ordered by the LORD: and he delighteth in his way. Though he fall, he shall not be utterly cast down: for the LORD upholdeth him with his hand" (Psalm 37:23-24).

No, there is no lion in the streets. But there are great opportunities for every person who will leave his excuses behind and step out on the promises of God.

Rather than allowing his mouth to defeat him by confessions of imaginary obstacles, a Christian can make his mouth be a powerful ally in gaining biblical prosperity and success:

This book of the law shall not depart out of thy mouth; but thou shalt meditate therein day and night, that thou mayest observe to do according to all that is written therein: for then thou shalt make thy way prosperous, and then thou shalt have good success (Joshua 1:8).

8

"Except the Lord Build The House"

hat was the key to the immense success of the Apostolic Church in the Book of Acts? At its birth, 3,120 were added. Many more thousands were added on a regular basis, until finally the Bible no longer even uses numbers. It simply says that the church multiplied.

Someone computed the minimum number of believers in the Jerusalem church at the end of the Book of Acts by adding the specific numbers mentioned and doing a minimum multiplication. From this study it appears that there were at least 80,000 people in the Jerusalem church.

Gimmicks, Gadgets, and Madison Avenue

Through the years, I have collected various books on "how to grow a church." Many pay lip service to prayer and fasting but spend most of their pages talking about advertising, canvassing, giveaways, and other promo-

tional techniques. In their quest for growth, many churches have run the gamut of everything from giving away
balloons, candy, watermelons, money, automobiles, and
bicycles to holding outdoor services and counting almost
everyone who passed by. In fact, some have said, "I'll do
anything to get people to church, as long as it isn't illegal,
immoral, or unethical."

Many of the Madison Avenue techniques will result
in increased numbers, at least for as long as they are in
use. They are of little value, however, unless they are
followed by something more substantial. Moreover, gim-
micks and gadgets are conspicuous in the New Testament
by their absence.

Unity: The New Testament Key to Growth

The church in the Book of Acts did not erect one
billboard, hand out one flier, give out a single piece of bub-
ble gum, or hand out a pocket comb imprinted with the
name and address of the Upper Room. The key to their
growth was much deeper than superficial promotional
techniques: its root went back to a prayer uttered by
Jesus.

In John 17, Jesus prayed for His disciples and those
who would believe on Him through the disciples' word.
The focus of His prayer was unity: "That they all may
be one; as thou, Father, art in me, and I in thee, that they
also may be one in us: that the world may believe that
thou hast sent me. And the glory which thou gavest me
I have given them; that they may be one, even as we are
one" (John 17:21-22).

There is no division in God. There is one God. His purposes, thoughts, and actions are one. He does not change. Moreover, there was no conflict between the humanity of Jesus and the divine Spirit that dwelt within Him. As a man, Jesus always cooperated with and submitted to the Father.

Jesus prayed that His followers would be one, even as He as a man was one with God. Jesus' prayer was answered: "And when the day of Pentecost was fully come, they were all with one accord in one place" (Acts 2:1).

This oneness, this unity of the 120, provided the right atmosphere for the outpouring of the Holy Ghost. The Holy Spirit, symbolized in Scripture as a dove, would not have visited a group of bickering, fighting, strife-filled people. Their unity paved the way for the arrival of the Holy Spirit, which in turn resulted in 3,000 being added to the church that very day.

Moreover, the Lord continued to add to the church daily (Acts 2:47). How did this continued growth occur? "And they, continuing daily with one accord in the temple, and breaking bread from house to house, did eat their meat with gladness and singleness of heart" (Acts 2:46). On the basis of their unity, God continued to add to the church.

Jesus prayed that we would be one so that the world would believe on Him (John 17:21). What a wonderful thing it is for a local group of believers when they take their eyes off mere numbers and competition long enough to examine their unity. In the long run, momentary, "hyped-up," Madison-Avenue growth will not bring peace and unity to a local church. Rather, genuine peace and unity will result in a biblical pattern of church growth.

107

The Purpose for Humanity on Earth

Why are humans on the earth? For what purpose did God create the magnificent human body, investing in it the qualities of creativity and intelligence? Is God pleased with human efforts to escape as much responsibility as possible? Is it God's idea for believers to maintain as low a profile as possible in the struggle to stay out of trouble until the rapture?

Many Christians answer the last two questions in the affirmative, with their lifestyle if not with their words. Some discourage Christian youth from obtaining a solid education. "The Lord is coming soon," they insist. "Going to school is a waste of time." Young men preparing for the ministry in Christian colleges are sometimes treated with similar fare: "You're fooling your time away. Get out and get busy."

Some sincere Christians even have the attitude that we should not attempt to stop abortion, squash pornography, bring inflation to a halt, or influence our society in any way. Though they do not express their desires vocally, their position is clearly shown by their uninvolvement and lethargy regarding anything that does not immediately concern them.

But God told Adam and Eve, "Be fruitful, and multiply, and replenish the earth, and subdue it" (Genesis 1:28). There is no escape mentality here. The commands are positive: be productive, increase your numbers, spread out over the earth, and rule it.

God repeated this mandate to Noah (Genesis 9:1).

Did God's purpose for righteous people change under the New Covenant? Jesus commanded, "All power is given unto me in heaven and in earth. Go ye therefore, and teach all nations, baptizing them . . . teaching them to observe all things whatsoever I have commanded you: and, lo, I am with you alway, even unto the end of the world" (Matthew 28:18-20).

Jesus Christ is Lord, and He has all power. Therefore, His disciples are to go, to teach (literally, disciple), to baptize, and to instruct all nations. The nations are to come under obedience to all that Jesus commanded. This is the New Covenant parallel of the mandate that God gave Adam and Noah in the Old Testament. The obligation of New Testament Christians is to subdue the world spiritually for Christ.

Admittedly, this is an ambitious project. It is a command, however, and God's commands are His enablements. In order to carry out the mandate, Christians must clean out the cobwebs of wrong thinking and allow the fresh breeze of God's sovereignty to clear their minds.

The first element of the mandate is power and authority. Obviously, power and authority are necessary to carry out this humanly impossible task. Jesus prefaced His command with the reassurance that He has all power and authority. Many Christians give enthusiastic lip service to this concept but do not act upon it.

God's power is real power and it does not just cover "religious" matters. Every ounce of power in the universe is in the hands of Jesus Christ. The devil has no power over Christians. He can only do what God permits him to do. God's plan is to subdue the earth and disciple the nations through the efforts of His followers. To a large degree, His followers have abdicated the world to the devil; this rebel has controlled as much as he has simply

109

by default.

If two baseball teams are scheduled to play and one fails to show up, the team that shows up wins, while the other forfeits the game. If both teams show up, but one refuses to put any players in the outfield, then the team that sends in players to cover every position will win. Even though God's power is greater than that of Satan, God's followers must actually use that power to implement God's will on earth.

The second element of the mandate has to do with mobility and visibility. "Go," Jesus said. This command is in direct opposition to the low-profile, uninvolved, hermitic mentality that many Christians display. Christians do not belong in a mountain cave drinking orange juice and keeping inventory on their stock of wheat. They belong in the thick of the battle, at the forefront. Not only should their churches sit on Main Street, but their members should sit on boards of education, in municipal offices, in state offices, and in national offices. In short, the salt needs to be taken off the shelf and sprinkled throughout society.

The third aspect of the mandate is educational in nature. The nations must be taught the Word of God, or made disciples of Christ. In order for someone to teach, he must first be taught. Inherent in the mandate is the requirement that Christ's followers learn. They must "go to school," whether formally or informally. Time spent in learning is never wasted. Children are included in those who must be taught. The church must teach them academically, socially, physically, and spiritually. In addition to teaching the Word, Christians should teach the Word's applications to all things.

The fourth part of Christ's commission has to do with bringing the nations under obedience to His commands. This begins with baptism, which is one of the first, elementary, tangible evidences that an individual is accepting the lordship of Christ. But it certainly does not end there. Jesus told His church to teach the nations "to observe all things whatsoever I have commanded you." In other words, the church must proclaim all of Christ's ministry. Beginning with baptism, people must be taught to observe, in every facet of life, all of the Lord's words, whether in the church, the factory, the schoolroom, the town hall, or the courtroom.

Finally, the Great Commission contains the promise of Christ's presence in all of the aforementioned endeavors. In other words, wherever His people go in response to His mandate, the Lord goes. If they step into the pulpit, He is there. If they stand at an assembly line, he is there. If they occupy a teacher's desk, He is there. If they stand in a courtroom in defense of Christian liberties, He is there. If they sit on a legislative council, He is there. And in each place, the Christian's task is to subdue, or apply God's Word to, the situation at hand, to lead people into conformity with divine principles, to be salt and light to the world.

God did not place people on earth for them to run and hide but to go and shine. The church is not to be the tail but the head. (See Deuteronomy 28:13.)

Humanism in the Church

Much that passes for God-centered religion these days is really man-centered humanism. Churches and sermons are often organized around the desires of people. Policies, programs, and facilities are designed for the convenience of people. There is an obvious attempt to lure people with Christian entertainment.

Some time ago, my wife and I stayed overnight in another city. While there, I perused the Yellow Pages for information on local churches. One church advertised, among other things, "Weddings, Funerals, Counseling." Some churches claim to be "The Finest Church in Town." Others assert that their's is the "Most Exciting Sunday School in Town." It is not uncommon to see churches, in such advertisements, boasting of their carpeted floors, padded pews, air conditioning, nursery attended by a paid professional staff, well lighted and guarded parking lot, and so forth.

Although these things are good in themselves and can be helpful to a church, emphasizing them and relying primarily on them is an appeal to the flesh. Such advertisements promote a people-centered religion rather than a God-centered faith.

Jesus did not lure followers by the promise of soft comfort. He said, "Foxes have holes, and birds of the air have nests; but the Son of man hath not where to lay his head" (Luke 9:58). He did not even offer a "family-centered" ministry. Instead, Jesus said, "Let the dead bury their dead" (Luke 9:60). One man was willing to follow Him, if he could first go home and tell his family goodbye. But Jesus said, "No man, having put his hand to the plough, and looking back, is fit for the kingdom of God" (Luke 9:62).

No, Jesus did not promise air conditioning and safe parking lots. Nor did He assure His disciples that He would conduct a dignified funeral in the event of their death. He told Peter that he would become a martyr. When Peter wanted to know if John would suffer the same fate, Jesus replied, "What is that to thee? follow thou me" (John 21:18-22). In other words, Jesus did not assure Peter that he would be treated fairly by temporal standards.

The church should not encourage people to pamper their flesh, but to deny the flesh. The church should not rely on promises of exciting entertainment, to attract and retain people, but it should draw them by the demand to take up the cross.

Except the LORD build the house, they labour in vain that build it (Psalm 127:1).

This verse does not deny that it is possible to build a house without the Lord's involvement; it simply says that such an effort is ultimately vain.

9

The Christian Citizen

From my childhood in northeast Arkansas and southeast Missouri, I remember clearly the courthouse "Spit and Whittle Club" as well as the group of men who gathered around the potbellied stove in my father's feed store. The most common topic of conversation for either group was governmental problems, from local to worldwide affairs. Amazingly, these fellows seemed to have all the answers and knew exactly what the governmental leaders should do.

I have no way of knowing how many of these men carried their alleged concern to the extreme of praying for their country, working for godly candidates, or voting. However, I am becoming more and more convinced that God's Word instructs Christians to become involved in the process of governing their country to the extent that the government allows citizen participation.

Render unto Caesar

The Pharisees, in one of their many attempts to en-

115

tangle Jesus, asked Him if it were right to pay taxes to Caesar, who was certainly not an example of godly government. Jesus put a stop to their efforts by pointing out that certain things belong to Caesar and certain things belong to God. (See Matthew 22:15-22.) He stated a principle developed further in Romans 13:1-8, which tells believers to render tribute (pay taxes), custom, fear, and honor. These were the things the Roman Empire asked of its citizens.

When the government asks for citizen participation, citizens should respond. Christian citizens are not to owe the government anything; that is, they are not to refrain from doing their duty.

The very first duty of Christians is God-given: they must pray for their leaders (I Timothy 2:1-3). Believers have no license to critize and complain, especially if they have not first prayed. If they pray regularly, they probably will not criticize.

The second civic duty is given by democracies: believers should register to vote and encourage other Christians to do the same. Believers miss an opportunity to be salt (preserving influence) and light (illumination of God's will and Word) if they do not use their influence in this matter. "By the blessing of the upright the city is exalted: but it is overthrown by the mouth of the wicked" (Proverbs 11:11).

The third duty is to become informed. Just as God's people are destroyed for a lack of knowledge of God's Word, so will a society be destroyed if it is ignorant of the decisions its government makes. Christians need to become informed about current issues that threaten religious freedom. It is much easier to work to prevent

116

a bad law from passing than to change it once it is on the books.

The fourth duty is to work to select and elect candidates who will act according to godly principles. "When the righteous are in authority, the people rejoice: but when the wicked beareth rule, the people mourn" (Proverbs 29:2). The first place to get involved is in the local area, the precinct. Many elections are won or lost by only one vote or less, on average, per precinct.

The fifth duty is to vote faithfully in every election for the best candidates, regardless of party. Many people think decisions are made by the majority. That is not true. Decisions are made by the majority of those who vote. As few as sixteen percent of all eligible voters in a district can elect a member of Congress. Presidents have been elected by an average of one-half vote per precinct nationwide. The responsibilities that citizens do not use, they lose. This has occurred many times over in many countries.

Christian citizens should fulfill their civic duties. They should pray, register to vote, become informed, work, and vote. When there is an election, their voice should be heard.

I was able to attend the gigantic "Washington for Jesus" rally some years ago, and my experience there prompted me to contemplate the nature of our national problems and the possible solutions to them. At the root of the various manifestations of turmoil is a cause. Whether the problem is abortion, secular humanism, "equal rights" for perversion, or any other of the myriad sores on our nation, there is one root cause: God's moral law has been broken. The moral posture of the nation is

117

becoming increasingly challenged.

A discussion of morality immediately leads most people to think of the more obvious sins such as adultery and fornication. And these are certainly a major part of the problem. But just as devastating, though less obvious, is the breakdown of honesty, integrity, and fairness.

Who is to blame for this problem? The church bears some responsibility, for Jesus said, "Ye are the salt of the earth. . . . ye are the light of the world. . . . Let your light so shine before men" (Matthew 5:13-16).

David Manuel, in his book *The Gathering,* a complete story of the "Washington for Jesus" rally, relates the story of a senator who was visited by four organizers of the rally:

The Senator stood and faced the four men who had come to his office. "America today is like a plane going down in flames," he said, pausing to let the words sink in. "I'm not a religious man, but you and your rally just may be our parachute." His smile passed quickly. "But I'll tell you one thing: the fact that we are going down in flames is not the fault of the politicians. Nor is it the fault of the economists or the so-called military-industrial complex. It's your fault," he said, pointing to each of the men present. "If the Church had been to this country what it should have been, we would not be in the shape we're in today."

What has the church been to this country during recent years? While it is dangerous to make sweeping statements, it appears that many Christians have retreated into a monastic attitude of uninvolvement with anything outside the immediate scope of local church activities. They have been more concerned with interchurch competition, chili suppers, building bigger barns, division, and debate than in salting the earth, lighting the world, and living in such a way that people see their good works and glorify God. Many have wanted only to be left alone, and they have looked askance at those who have tried to influence government for righteousness. Regularly they repeat the old adage: Religion and politics don't mix.

The truth is that a politician will either abide by Christian principles or not. In the beginning of the nation, most of them did, at least to the extent of their understanding.

George W. Cornell, writing for The Associated Press in an article that appeared on Saturday, July 4, 1987, in *The Stockton Record,* pointed out that faith in God and a sense of responsibility to Him strongly influenced the birth of the United States of America:

"Although modern commentators sometimes argue about whether religion should have anything to do with politics, it was a religious concept that produced the nation itself.

"That transcendent principle was the backbone of a document celebrated on July 4—the Declaration of Independence—which initiated the very nationhood that gives politics its life.

"The declaration 'ought to be commemorated as the day of deliverance, by solemn acts of devotion to Almighty God,' wrote John Adams, one of its signers who became prevailing theory that kings inherited divine rule.

"The justification that it sets forth for the birth of these United States was that human beings are 'endowed by their Creator with certain inalienable Rights' that cannot be usurped by any other power. They belong inherently to people, rights derived from the 'Laws of Nature and Nature's God,' the declaration says, and they cannot be given nor taken away by any monarch or government.

"On that basis, hinged to that high conviction, and 'appealing to the Supreme Judge of the World for the Rectitude of Our intentions,' the founding fathers declared the independence of the 13 British colonies.

"In doing so, they asserted their 'firm Reliance on the Protection of divine Providence.' Four times in that brief, ringing exposition of the cause for independence, the founders rested their case on God.

"The signers were all religious men. Some of them such as Benjamin Franklin and Thomas Jefferson were called 'deists,' who had little use for denominational rivalries and who considered their faith reasonable Christianity.

" 'Deism' generally consisted of affirmations that God created and sustained the natural world, that he is to be worshipped, that worship demands virtue, that wrongdoing should be repented and that there is an afterlife of rewards and punishments. . . .

"As for denominational affiliations, the 56 signers of the declaration included 30 Anglicans (Episcopalians), 12 Congregationalists, seven Presbyterians, 4 Quakers, one Baptist, one Unitarian and one Roman Catholic. . . .

"The Continental Congress regularly opened its sessions with prayer, a practice still continued by the U.S.

Congress.

"In drafting the constitution . . . debate over it had virtually ground to a standstill in mid-summer of 1787, bogged down in wrangling conflict.

"It was an 'awful and critical moment,' wrote William Few, a Georgia delegate, who said if the impasse was not resolved, the 'dissolution of the union of states seemed inevitable.'

"In that crisis, Benjamin Franklin, 81, the oldest of the delegates, took the floor, suggesting an humble 'applying to the Father of Lights to illuminate our understanding.'

"We have been assured, sir, in the sacred Writings, that 'except the Lord build the house, they labor in vain that build it,' " he added. 'I have lived a long time, sir, and the longer I live, the more convincing proofs I see of this truth—that God governs in the affairs of men.

" 'I firmly believe that, and I also believe that without his concurring aid, we shall succeed in this political building not better than the builders of the tower of Babel.'

"In the ensuing discussion, Edmund Randolph of Virginia proposed a special sermon be preached on July 4, and from then on, there be daily intercessory prayers. It was done, and on Sept. 17, 1787, the Constitution was approved.

"George Washington, who served as the first president, said, 'Of all the dispositions and habits which lead to political prosperity, religion and morality are indispensable supports.'

"Religion, said Jefferson, is the 'alpha and omega of the moral law' and 'a supplement to law in the government of men.'

"Alexis de Tocqueville, a French statesman and historian commissioned to analyze the special genius of the American system in its early stages, termed religion 'the foremost of their political institutions.'"

Why are not more God-fearing men working in government or influencing government today? If the salt loses its saltiness, it is good for nothing but to be thrown out and trodden under foot. If a light is placed under a bushel, it is only of benefit to those who crawl under the bushel with it.

If Christians fail in their responsibility of preserving righteousness and illuminating the darkness, then they must share the blame for unrighteousness and darkness. They need the forgiveness of God and a turn back to morality, with all its implications.

The reason why believers should pray for kings and for all who are in authority is that "we may lead a quiet and peaceable life in all godliness and honesty" (I Timothy 2:2). The prayerlessness of Christians can be a cause of much social unrest.

Christians in Government

In recent years an increasing number of Christians are rising to a new awareness of their responsibilities to God and country. They are laying hold on their duty to be "the sons of God . . . in the midst of a crooked and perverse nation, among whom ye shine as lights in the world; holding forth the word of life" (Philippians 2:15-16).

Many Christians in the past have been content to let their light shine in the church building, in their neighborhoods, at work, or at school, not realizing that they should place no limitation on where the light should shine. Most have given little thought to letting their light shine in the halls of Congress, in the courtrooms, and in the executive branch of government.

If a person sings, "I'll go where you want me to go, I'll do what you want me to do, I'll say what you want me to say, and I'll be what you want me to be," or if he prays, "Not my will, but thine be done," he must remove all limitations. He must be willing not only for God to send him to the steaming jungles but also to the statehouses. He must not only be willing to declare God's law to his next-door neighbor but also to governmental leaders, as did John the Baptist and the Apostle Paul.

Christians who are awakening to a broader view of their responsibilities face pressure from two widely opposing forces. First, they face the bitter frowns of some liberal politicians, who have much to lose if the vast majority of Americans who hold to traditional moral values are ever galvanized into action. Not surprisingly, these people welcome the input of the Christian community as long as its views are in harmony with those they espouse. But when the views held by the majority of God-fearing people conflict with the secular element, as they often do, great howls of protest go up, and churches and preachers are accused of unfairly using their tax-exempt status and pulpits. Alert Christians can easily handle this criticism, because it is obviously biased and a response to the raising up of godly standards.

The second source of pressure comes from other sincere Christians who are convinced that their brothers and sisters are dead wrong to meddle in government.

These pressures are more intense, for they are from within rather than without. Confusion results as those caught in between struggle to find the biblical ground.

And dangers do exist in the political process. While Christians should seek to influence their nation in godly ways, they cannot become involved in any political action or hold any government position that would require them to compromise biblical convictions. Moreover they should not allow civic activities to deflect them from the church's central mission of evangelism, nor should they use political power to promote the church.

Several false concepts have confused the issue of Christian participation in government. The separation of church and state, a phrase not found in the Constitution or Bill of Rights but coined by Thomas Jefferson, has been reinterpreted to mean "separation of God and state." This was not what Jefferson had in mind. Separation of church and state simply means that the state cannot establish an official church and that the church, as an institution, cannot rule the state. What many seem to forget is that the church is made up of individuals who are also citizens of the state. A person does not become a second-class citizen when he becomes a Christian. Rather, his responsibility to influence his country for good is greater than ever before. Believers are not to be overcome with evil, but they are to overcome evil with good (Romans 12:21).

In any case, Jefferson first used the phrase "a wall of separation between church and state" many years after the writing of the Constitution. Jefferson, who composed the Declaration of Independence, had nothing to do with the writing of the Constitution; he was overseas at the time. Subsequently, when he was running for a political office, Christian people opposed him because he was a Deist. In his exasperation over the opposition of the preachers, he said in a personal letter to a friend, "There should be a wall of separation between church and state."

The current popular view of the "separation of church and state" is a misinterpretation of the First Amendment to the Constitution, found in the Bill of Rights. Here is what the First Amendment actually says:

> Congress shall make no law respecting an establishment of religion, or prohibiting the free exercise thereof; or abridging the freedom of speech, or of the press; or the right of the people peaceably to assemble, and to petition the government for a redress of grievances.

There is no mention of the church. There is no mention of the state. There is no mention of a wall. There is no mention of separation.

Actually the First Amendment was designed to prevent the federal government (Congress) from passing any law regarding establishment of religion, or in any way prohibiting the free exercise of religion. In no way does the First Amendment affect a Christian's involvement in government. It merely prevents the federal government from dictating to the people a national religion, and it forbids the same government to tamper in any way with an individual's freedom to exercise his own religious faith.

The Constitution in no way suggests that Christians should have no influence in government. In fact, the Founding Fathers were, for the most part, believers in the Bible.

There is also a common misunderstanding of the scriptural position on believer's involvement in governmental affairs. Time and again the Scripture records the influence of godly people in their governments.

Moses, a civil and religious leader, wrote the first five books of the Bible. The sixth book, Joshua, is the story of the man who took his place. Judges concerns the succession of civil rulers God raised up for Israel. Samuel was both a prophet of God and a civil ruler. I and II Kings and I and II Chronicles concern the histories of the civil rulers of Israel, some of whom were more godly than others. Ezra, Nehemiah, and Esther all chronicle the story of men and women who were civil or political leaders and who exerted a godly influence. The bulk of the Psalms were written by David, a king. A king, Solomon, also penned Proverbs, Ecclesiastes, and the Song of Solomon. The prophets Isaiah, Jeremiah, and Ezekiel were called primarily to proclaim God's Word to the leaders of their generation. Daniel was a vice-president in a pagan government. Jonah declared the mind of God to Nineveh, a powerful political entity in his day. Like the major prophets, the minor prophets were commissioned to preach God's will to the people and their governments.

Even in the New Testament, which does not provide many details about the personal lives of early Christians, Paul mentioned "Erastus the chamberlain of the city" (Romans 16:23). This governmental position was a very responsible one; Erastus was the city treasurer. To the church at Philippi, Paul said, "All the saints salute you, chiefly they that are of Caesar's household" (Philippians 4:22).

In addition to the responsibilities to pray, register,

get informed, work, and vote, a Christian should be available if it is God's will to serve Him in public office. It will do no good to excuse uninvolvement by saying, "There are too many crooks in politics." There are also plenty of crooked truck drivers, retail clerks, farmers, bank tellers, salesmen, and executives. This does not excuse the Christian from fulfilling God's call.

The erroneous notion that Christians are not to "dirty their hands" with governmental affairs must be laid to rest. If the system is dirty, believers must pitch in and clean it up. It would be wrong to abandon any area of society prior to the coming of Christ. Until the very moment of His appearing, Christians must exert their utmost to "occupy."

After the Election, Then What?

"Let us remember that when the dust from the election has settled and the last vote is counted, our final destiny does not rest with the men who go to Washington, but with the Man who went to the cross. His kingdom will prevail."

The above words from a Christian magazine struck a responsive chord in my heart. Christians are to exert their influence in the political and governmental arena, just as they are to be "salt" and "light" in every area of human existence. They should do everything within their ability to elect people who will act upon biblical principles. They should get to know their leaders in order to influence them in godly ways. A person in a position of influence can be even more powerful than one in a position of authority.

But regardless of who is in office, God is in control. Even if the ruler is ungodly, believers should pray for him. "The king's heart is in the hand of the LORD, as the rivers of water: he turneth it whithersoever he will" (Proverbs 21:1). God makes the final decision as to who is in authority. "And he changeth the times and the seasons: he removeth kings, and setteth up kings" (Daniel 2:21). Several times in Scripture pagan kings are said to be God's servants fulfilling His will.

Since it has often been the will of God for His people to serve in positions of civil authority and influence, Christians today should be available to Him for a similar ministry. Bible-believing people should be heard more and more, so that skeptics will not have unchallenged access to the decision-making apparatus of the nation.

Thankfully, there are Christians willing to put works with their faith. Such a combination gives life and could very well result in freedoms being renewed and extended to give the church further opportunities to reach the billions who have never yet been saved.

May today's believers never reach the state that the ancient Israelites did. God had promised that He would spare an evil nation if the people would repent. But their response was, "There is no hope: but we will walk after our own devices" (Jeremiah 18:12).

There is hope. It is always too soon to give up.

10

Training up a Child

Train up a child in the way he should go: and when he is old, he will not depart from it (Proverbs 22:6).

Nation's Business, a magazine that has no particular axe to grind on the subject, predicted that by 1990 public schools would play a minor role in the total educational scene, because an increasing number of parents are withdrawing their children from government schools to enroll them in private schools or to teach them at home. Rousas J. Rushdoony has pointed out that, should present trends continue, by the year 2,000 every student in America would be attending a private, church-related school.

Public education is actually government education. As an apologist for government schools, Temple University demographer Joseph McFalls wrote in an article entitled "When 'Families' Will Have a New Definition" (*U.S. News and World Report,* May 9, 1983), "Although this sounds like science fiction, it's really not so unusual for one institution, such as the family, to give up some of its functions to another, such as the government. . . . Families used to be responsible for the education of children and the care of the aged; the government does both now."

There is a tension today between humanistic scholars and activists who propose and predict a restructuring of the family, and the conservative Christian community, which is working hard to reestablish biblical priorities. One of the battlegrounds is the field of education.

While it is extremely doubtful that government education would ever be abolished in our country (though some eminent politicians and philosophers have suggested just such a move), it appears that a significant trend is currently underway. Is Christian education just another fad that will pass in time? Is the Christian school and home school movement a bandwagon that will finally run its course, leaving vacated classrooms and ending with a reverse exodus back to the governmental system? Or is it the result of a genuine desire to educate youth in accordance with the principles of God's Word, which is destined to be a part of the church until the end?

I am firmly convinced that many Christian schools have been founded in response to a definite unction of the Holy Spirit. Many pastors and parents across the country are suffering for their conviction that their children must be in Christian schools. If this were simply another fad, they would abandon it as soon as they met official opposition.

Christian education certainly has a scriptural foundation. "Beware lest any man spoil you through philosophy and vain deceit, after the tradition of men, after the rudiments of the world, and not after Christ" (Colossians 2:8). "Blessed is the man that walketh not in the counsel of the ungodly, nor standeth in the way of sinners, nor sitteth in the seat of the scornful. But his delight is in the law of the LORD; and in his law doth he meditate day and night" (Psalm 1:1-2). "Cease, my son, to hear the instruction that causeth to err from the words of knowledge" (Proverbs 19:27).

Many people in the Christian education movement are involved because of conviction, not preference. It is not always the easiest, cheapest, and most convenient thing in the world for them to do. They do it because they want to train children in the ways of God.

Opportunities for Youth

One of the keys to the progress of God's work is to train youth and involve increasing numbers of them in productive, full-time Christian ministry. The church should encourage young people to see the many areas of full-time service available to them, even if they are not called to the preaching ministry. The challenge God has set before the local church is more than any one person can meet. The combined efforts of many people are necessary, each working together for a common goal, under the leadership and authority of the pastor.

We see this principle in Acts 6, where the staff was not sufficient to meet the needs of "the daily ministration." The twelve apostles recognized that it was not reasonable for them to leave the Word of God to serve tables, so they made arrangements for other spiritual men to care for that task, while they gave themselves continually to prayer and to the ministry of the Word. Had the Twelve not risen to this challenge, the church in Jerusalem would surely have suffered serious strife and would very likely have disintegrated. Similar situations present themselves today, and they can result either in great progress or in backward movement.

Let us discuss some of the splendid opportunities for youth to engage in full-time Christian ministry in the near future.

Christian education. At the present, it is estimated that there are as many as six hundred Christian schools within the United Pentecostal Church International. These schools are calling for qualified faculty. Here is an opportunity for Christian youth with a desire to invest their lives in a meaningful way to enter full-time ministry, though they may not be called to preach. The full spectrum of Christian educators is needed, including those majoring in each discipline. The wise young person who has an interest in training others will begin now to qualify for this opportunity. Some of our endorsed colleges have already seen the need to offer programs to those interested in entering this field.

Music. Increasing numbers of churches are coming to see the importance of music in the local church. David established a pattern of worship that made extensive use of music. He assigned certain people to sing and to play as their sole responsibility. In fact, David made about four thousand musical instruments to be used in worship.

Music is an undeniable part of worship, and as such it deserves attention in order to achieve the highest possible quality. It is not unscriptural to employ someone full-time to work with the ministry of music. The duties of this individual could include directing a choir, arranging various vocal and instrumental numbers, teaching music to interested members, and working with other ministries of the church to provide the highest possible quality of music for outreach programs, street meetings, nursing homes, schools, and so on. Many churches already have such music directors, and more will be looking for them. Most of our colleges now provide good training programs for those who wish to enter this ministry.

Missions. The door is beginning to open for various types of short-term and long-term ministries on the foreign fields other than preaching. Some fields operate elementary and secondary schools, and there is a need for qualified people to help establish such schools, train staff, and be available for continuing oversight. Most fields now have Bible schools and need Bible teachers. Another possibility is for someone with a skill in a particular area to travel from field to field, working and training others in that skill. It might be carpentry, communications, graphic arts, or music. There are many ways to lighten a missionary's load and to help nations upgrade their skills, just as in North America.

Preaching. The foregoing discussion does not minimize the role of the preacher. The pastor has the final spiritual responsibility for a congregation, and all others must work in harmony with him and under his direction. But as the foreign and home missions divisions have stressed, while money is needful, the most urgent need is for people to commit themselves totally to the will of God. Preaching, teaching, evangelizing, and pastoring may have very little glamor, but they are extremely rewarding. Any young person who senses that God is dealing with him about this type of ministry should not close the door but should pursue his call. Established churches need good pastors, and multitudes still await a truth-proclaiming church in their area.

Writing. While writing may not yet be a full-time ministry, it may very well be in the near future. In the meantime, those who have skills in the area of written communication should work to polish that ability by submitting articles to the various publications presently in existence and even to other Christian publishers. We need books written from the Pentecostal viewpoint; we should pursue this field just as vigorously as other groups do. We must never underestimate the power of the printed word. A writing ministry can also work in conjunction with missions, as the need for Pentecostal curriculum and materials in other languages increases.

Administration. More and more churches are recognizing the need to relieve the pastor of unnecessary administrative details by giving those responsibilities to people called of God to function in that area. The description of spiritual gifts mentions the gifts of "helps" and "governments" (I Corinthians 12:28). These ministries must work under the authority and direction of the pastor, but he needs to be free from the day-to-day pressure of paperwork, computer terminals, and ledgers, just as the apostles freed themselves from the need to wait on tables every day (Acts 6). Those with skills in budgeting, accounting, and computers should examine the possibility of exercising their expertise in the church.

Law. As the courts decide an increasing number of issues that concern Christian freedoms, it becomes more apparent that well qualified Christian attorneys are needed. Such people would have more than an academic or professional interest in the issues at hand. A very small number of attorneys have devoted themselves to the defense of Christian liberties, but the proliferation of cases is so great that they operate on the thin edge of exhaustion and financial disaster. In recent years the judicial system has become more and more a determiner of future trends. The Christian voice should be strongly heard where momentous decisions are being made.

There is definitely a place for youth in God's church. There is a place for anyone willing to follow His call and to do His will.

11

A Look at the Future

From the time that iniquity was found in Lucifer, he has had a conspiracy to overthrow the kingdom of God. His efforts have taken many forms and involved multitudes of people, including world leaders in both the political and religious realms.

But it is certain that Satan will never be successful in his diabolical schemes. His fate is already sealed. He is already defeated. All of his grandiose and elaborately conceived plans are weak and pitiful. It matters not how many men in high places are on his side. It makes no difference how much wealth he has access to. All of Satan's efforts will one day be swept away by the brightness of the coming of the Lord Jesus Christ.

We are living in the last days. The Bible describes the increasing growth of turmoil and evil during this time, and we can see the fulfillment of its prophecies in our day.

However, the reaction of some Christians to prophecies of doom is a cause for concern. Some have confused prophecy with fate. Succumbing to the idea that no one can do anything to affect the course of the future, many Christians have abdicated their God-given responsibilities. In fact, some have gone so far as to return to the monastic concept of the Dark Ages. But it was never God's will for His people to hole up in a cave or retreat to the wilderness to flee a coming calamity.

Instead, it is God's will for His people to be actively involved in declaring the Word of God, offering the solution, right until the very last possible moment of repentance. God commanded Isaiah to declare His Word even though there was apparently no hope of revival. When Isaiah asked the Lord how long he should continue in that fruitless pursuit, the Lord replied that he should minister until the land was forsaken. (See Isaiah 6.)

It is disturbing to see so many Christians today give eager ears to prophecies of doom, swallowing them up in an indiscriminating fashion and willingly accepting the most dire predictions as accurate. Indeed, many get more excited about this kind of news than they have ever gotten about the good news of the gospel. There almost seems to be a thirst for the spectacular, a sort of weird desire that strangely hopes the worst is true.

Jesus predicted perilous times. But He said those who hear of these things should not be troubled (Matthew 24:6). False prophets who emphasize doom but who do not proclaim the gospel have always abounded. They were at work even before the New Testament was complete. In reaction to the effects of such fear mongers at Thessalonica, Paul wrote, "Be not soon shaken in mind, or be troubled, neither by spirit, nor by word, nor by letter as from us, as that the day of Christ is at hand"

(II Thessalonians 2:2).

When a message is troubling or mentally disturbing, believers should be wary of it, whether it comes cloaked in a great spiritual disguise or whether it comes by word or by letter. God does not give a spirit of fear. His gift is a spirit of power, and of love, and of a sound mind (II Timothy 1:7). Anything that breeds weakness, hatred, or confusion is of Satan, not God. God does not move people with suspicion and base passion. He is not the author of confusion.

Believers should spend their valuable time in the pure Word of God. They should study the prophecies of God's Word and proclaim the message of coming judgment as well as salvation, but they must leave speculation and idle predictions to others. God has promised protection, provision, and power to those who dwell in His secret place (Psalm 91).

Secret Things

The sin of Adam and Eve involved seeking forbidden knowledge. The Lord God commanded Adam not to eat of the tree of the knowledge of good and evil. According to Deuteronomy 29:29 some knowledge is still hidden from humanity: "The secret things belong unto the LORD our God: but those things which are revealed belong unto us and to our children for ever."

However, human nature is curious and inquisitive. If people think there is something they do not know—particularly if it is supposedly secret information—they are eager to search it out. This carries over into the realm of the spiritual.

Mark 13:32 identifies a definite area of hidden knowledge: "But of that day and that hour knoweth no man, no, not the angels which are in heaven, neither the Son, but the Father." According to the context and a consideration of Matthew 24 and Luke 21, this verse speaks of the Second Advent—the return of the Lord.

The interpretation that some people place on these passages could lead one to believe that Christ's appearing can be pinpointed to a precise time. The disciples did ask, "When shall these things be? and what shall be the sign of thy coming, and of the end of the world" (Matthew 24:3). Jesus did not tell them specifically when He would return, however, as Matthew 24:36-51, Mark 13:32-37, and Luke 21:34-36 show.

What about Matthew 24:30, Mark 13:26, and Luke 21:27? The first of these declares that following the darkening of the sun and moon, "then shall appear the sign of the Son of man in heaven," and the other two say basically the same thing. It is important to recognize that the word *then* as used here does not necessarily mean "immediately." It usually refers to the order, rather than the time, of events. It speaks of transition.

The Lord Jesus did not utter words in vain. Each word He used had a precise purpose. In Matthew 24:29, He used the word *eutheos,* which is translated "immediately," meaning "at once, or soon." Surely, if He had meant that His appearing would follow immediately on the heels of the events mentioned in verse 29, He would have used the same word again, just a few words later. Instead, He used *tote,* translated "then," which suggests that His appearing would be the next significant event but gives no hint as to precisely when it would come. If no one can accurately predict the time of the Second Advent, which will follow the Great Tribulation and precede the Millenium, it is equally impossible to predict the time of the rapture of the church.

The point is, the time of Christ's appearing is simply unknowable. It is a secret thing known only to God. Puny attempts to fit His grand design into our human schedules is laughable at best and dangerous at worst.

People have regularly predicted His appearing. The latest series of predictions that I have heard forecast His coming by the fall of 1980, sometime during 1982, at least by 1986, and—as someone said—"by 1993, or you'll wish He had come!"

Even though the time of His coming is clearly secret, some argue that they cannot know the day or hour, but that they can discern the season well enough to identify the specific year. However, this contention places an unwarranted literalism on Jesus' words. He did not mean merely that no one can know the twenty-four-hour period or the sixty-minute period in which He will return. The Greek word translated "day" carries the same general meaning as the English word "day," and is translated variously as "age, while, year." The word rendered "hour" is also translated "day, instant, season." The simple truth is that no one is able to pinpoint the time of the Lord's return.

His coming is imminent, but it is dangerous to make dogmatic statements, especially to predict dates. The motive may be noble (i.e., to save souls), but the end does not justify the means. Moreover, what happens to the credibility of a preacher who makes a prediction that fails to come to pass?

The church should eagerly look forward to and prepare for the soon coming of Jesus Christ. While we can identify the signs of the end time, we cannot know exactly when He will appear. As we wait for Him, let us not neglect our responsibilities to influence our world in godly ways. Even as we warn the world of coming destruction and judgment, let us proclaim the message of hope and salvation until the last moment.

12

Balance

One of the most valuable qualities a Christian can develop is balance. It is so easy and so common for someone to swing from one side of the pendulum to another, never striking the central stance of Scripture.

For example, Christians must balance love, which believes all things, with discernment, which believes not every spirit. (See I Corinthians 13:7 and I John 4:1.)

I am as thrilled as anyone about the move of the Spirit of God in the world today, and my basic philosophy is to accept a person's testimony at face value. I am not a skeptic, and I want to think that most of what people attribute to God is really of Him. However, uncritical acceptance can sometimes lead to disaster, and thus we see the importance of balance.

Even when God was inspiring men to write the Scriptures, there were false prophets among the people (II Peter 1:21; 2:9). Peter pointed out that, in like manner, there will always be false teachers in the midst of the Christian church. These false teachers (1) bring in damnable heresies; (2) deny the Lord that bought them; and (3) bring upon themselves swift destruction. Even though their teaching is false and they are destined for sure defeat, many people will follow their pernicious ways, causing the way of truth to be spoken of as evil.

These false teachers operate out of a basic motive of coveteousness and speak words that make merchandise of the people. Peter stressed their certain judgment as he recalled how God did not spare the sinful angels, the world in Noah's day, or the cities of Sodom and Gomorrah.

In summary, II Peter 2:9 states that God knows how to deliver the godly and He knows how to reserve the unjust unto the day of judgment.

Believers are safe from the deception of false teachers only as long as they stand firmly on the changeless, inspired, infallible Word of God, never bending from it for the sake of popularity, personality, acceptance, or friendship. They must derive balance and stability from God's Word.

13

The Sin of Murmuring

Murmuring is a sin that comes so naturally to so many, including Christians, that people often practice it without a thought as to its seriousness. Some may say, "Well, if it is a sin, it is just a little one—certainly not as bad as killing and stealing and all those other terrible things."

The Scripture teaches, however, that murmuring is a dangerous sin. It will keep a person from enjoying God's best, and it places him in the category of an ungodly sinner.

The Hebrew and Greek words that are translated "murmur" essentially mean "to grumble."

The Israelites were notorious for their murmuring, grumbling, and complaining. They grumbled for water, bread, and meat (Exodus 15-17). When they could not believe God for the Promised Land, they murmured and wept (Numbers 14). Their grumbling became a self-fulfilling prophecy and brought on them exactly what they feared (Numbers 14:27-28). When the Lord judged Korah and his cohorts by causing the earth to swallow them up, the Israelites complained against Moses and Aaron and sympathized with the sinners (Numbers 16:41).

Significantly, much of their murmuring took place in their tents, corrupting their children, so that God could spare only those under twenty. The older children had evidently heard so much complaining that they followed the same example.

Complaining was not just an Old Testament phenomenon. Many New Testament characters were just as practiced at it. The disciples murmured against the woman who anointed Jesus with an expensive ointment (Mark 14:5). The scribes and Pharisees were great grumblers and practiced their art against Jesus' disciples (Luke 5:30). The claims Jesus made prompted the Jews to murmur against Him (John 6:41).

Murmuring occurred even after Pentecost. The Grecians in the church murmured against the Hebrews because of the neglect of their widows (Acts 6:1).

What lesson should Christians learn about murmuring? "Neither murmur ye, as some of them also murmured, and were destroyed of the destroyer" (I Corinthians 10:10). Just as the rudder on a ship turns the huge vessel and the bit in the horse's mouth directs the large beast, so the tongue, though it is small, dictates the direction a person's life will take. (See James 3.) When the Israelites grumbled against God and expressed their fears, God gave them exactly what they confessed.

Shortly after speaking of the magnificence of the name of Jesus, Paul said, "Do all things without murmurings and disputings" (Philippians 2:14). In fact, God's

Word identifies a murmurer with the ungodly sinner: "Ungodly sinners have spoken against him. These are murmurers, complainers" (Jude 15–16).

Without a doubt, murmuring is a root sin that causes strife, division, and turmoil, and even splits churches. Spiritually, a tongue out of control is more dangerous than an atomic bomb or chemical warfare. Both "death and life are in the power of the tongue" (Proverbs 18:21), and only a fool says everything he thinks (Proverbs 29:11).

Christians must not be guilty of the destructive sin of murmuring. Instead they should use the power of the tongue to express thanksgiving, gratefulness, and praise.

The Value of Memorials

How many citizens of the United States of America observe Memorial Day according to its original intent? Originally designed to honor those who died in the Civil War, Memorial Day has subsequently been expanded to honor all the war dead.

Obviously, observance of that day will do little to benefit those who have already given their lives, but it should do something for those who observe it. When people consider the great price of war, they should be encouraged to take whatever steps are necessary to avoid it in the future.

What is the price of war? When World War I was finished, about ten million soldiers, plus an equal number of civilians, had paid the supreme price by giving their lives. Another twenty million were wounded, and an additional twenty million died from war-related epidemics and famines. That war cost world governments 338 billion dollars. It was, they said, the war to end all wars.

But it was not. When the horrors of World War II were assessed, seventeen million military dead and forty-three million civilian dead made the cost in human lives just about double that of World War I. About 1.348 trillion dollars had been expended in the conflict.

Memorial Day should be utilized to recall the terrific price war that exacts, to honor those who paid that price, and to resolve to take all necessary steps to lessen the likelihood of such carnage in the future.

In a spiritual sense, memorials are very powerful and can aid in living an overcoming life. They also provide a natural opportunity to teach children and to witness to others of God's power. Let us examine some memorials in the Bible.

1. The Passover (Exodus 12:14). As long as the Israelites observed this memorial, it reminded them that God makes a way of escape for His children by protecting them from harm. Jewish tradition dictated that on Passover night the youngest son would ask the father, "What makes this night different from all the rest?" This gave the father a natural opportunity to testify to God's care for His own.

2. The pot of manna (Exodus 16:31). This memorial taught two lessons. First, God will always supply the basic needs of His children. Second, a miracle is permanent, for the manna in the pot stayed fresh.

3. The fringes (Numbers 15:37-41). As a string tied around one's finger lest he forget something important, the fringes and blue ribbons on the borders of the Israelites' garments reminded them of God's laws and warned them from turning away.

4. The censers (Numbers 16:36-40). This memorial is

most interesting, for the censers had been instruments of sin and rebellion in the hands of Korah and his cohorts. However, they were beaten into another shape and made into coverings for the altar. This memorial served to remind the Israelites of the dangers of rebellion, for each time they saw the covers they would remember Korah and his destruction.

5. *The twelve stones (Joshua 4:1-7).* As the Israelites crossed the Jordan River, which God had parted miraculously, they picked up twelve stones from the riverbed in order to construct a memorial on the other side. Every time they saw that memorial in the future, it reminded them that God can make a way where there seems to be no way.

6. *The stone of witness (Joshua 24:24-27).* After reminding the Israelites of God's law, Joshua asked if they were willing to keep it. They promised to do so, and he set up a stone under an oak tree as a memorial. Each time they saw it, they were reminded of their vow to keep the Word of God.

7. *The Lord's Supper (Luke 22:17-20; I Corinthians 11:23-26).* Instituted by the Lord Jesus Himself, this memorial reminds believers of His shed blood and broken body, which were given for us.

When God performs a special work in someone's life, it is worthwhile for him to make some kind of memorial. First, this memorial will help him never to forget what God has done. Second, it will give him an opportunity to teach his children, grandchildren, and others who ask, "What does this mean?" According to Deuteronomy 4:9, each man is responsible for teaching his children and grandchildren. One of the greatest enemies of remembering God's deeds is prosperity (Deuteronomy 6:10-12).

It is beneficial for Christians to consider prayerfully those events for which they can establish memorials in their lives in a practical way. The Bible indicates that the following memorials are particularly helpful:

A memorial to God's protection

A memorial to God's Word

A memorial to God's supply

A memorial to the danger of rebellion

A memorial to God's making a way when there seemed to be no way

A memorial to vows made to God

A memorial of the price Jesus paid

15

Sources of Inner Conflict

One of the divine laws is the law of cause and effect. Things do not happen by accident; reaping is directly related to sowing (Galatians 6:7). "As the bird by wandering, as the swallow by flying, so the curse causeless shall not come" (Proverbs 26:2). One of the classic questions when calamity strikes is why? Those upon whom disaster falls often search in vain for a reason and sometimes even conclude by blaming God.

Sometimes trouble comes from Satan, as in the trial of Job, and sometimes it comes from ungodly people, as in the persecution of the Early Church. And God allows trials to test our faith and to purify us (I Peter 1:6-7; 4:12-13). Often, however, our own attitudes and actions are the source of trouble.

There is a definite relationship between conflict and the breaking of divine principles. When a person applies wisdom and understanding to areas of conflict in his life, it is possible for him to trace his problem to its root cause.

There are eight basic areas in which violation of God's principles will result in conflict.[1] Let us examine these areas in the form of personal questions.

1. Commitment to Christ. Have I been born again? Have I presented myself to God as a living sacrifice? Am I a channel of God's love to others?

2. Acceptance of Self. If I were standing in front of a mirror and were given the power to change anything about myself, would I use it? Have I learned to accept the way God made me. Am I thankful for the way God made me? Have I learned to be reconciled to, work with, and even attach meaning to unchangeable "defects"?

3. Harmony with Authority. God has ordained four basic structures of authority: family, church, government, and business. Am I sensitive and obedient to the wishes of those in authority over me? Do I show deference to their ideas?

4. Clear Conscience. Sometimes there is something more urgent than prayer. Jesus said, "Therefore, if thou bring thy gift to the altar, and there rememberest that thy brother hath ought against thee; leave there thy gift before the altar, and go thy way; first be reconciled to thy brother, and then come and offer thy gift" (Matthew 5:23-24). Have I asked forgiveness of all those whom I have offended, and have I made restitution wherever necessary or possible?

5. Spirit of Forgiveness. In teaching His disciples to pray, Jesus said, "And forgive us our debts, as we forgive our debtors" (Matthew 6;12). In explaining this principle He further stated, "For if ye forgive men their trespasses, your heavenly Father will also forgive you: but if ye forgive not men their trespasses, neither will

154

your Father forgive your trespasses" (Matthew 6:14-15). Have I forgiven all those who have offended me? Have I yielded all my personal "rights" to God? Do I know how to respond to sources of irritation?

6. Moral Freedom. Have I learned self-discipline, especially in my thought life? Is my personal and moral behavior above reproach? Have I learned to walk in God's Spirit and meditate on God's Word?

7. Purpose in Life. Do I have clearly defined goals that are related to the work and reputation of Christ? The Lord said to Jeremiah, "Before I formed thee in the belly I knew thee; and before thou camest out of the womb I sanctified thee, and I ordained thee a prophet unto the nations" (Jeremiah 1:5). "God is no respecter of persons" (Acts 10:34). He did not have a plan just for Jeremiah, but He has one for each of us.

8. Financial Principles. Have I dedicated my possessions, time, money, and earning power to God? Am I diligent and wise in my work and my use of money?

It is possible to trace almost every inner conflict to a violation of one or more of these principles. By applying God's Word in these areas, Christians will enjoy inner peace and victory under all circumstances.

Note

The author is indebted to the Institute in Basic Youth Conflicts for the eight principles in this chapter and for much insight on each one.

16

God's Three Requirements

What are God's absolute requirements? What must someone do to please Him? While the readers of this book will not want to stop with the minimum, before a person can go the second mile, he must complete the first.

The people who please God are not those who see how much they can be like the world and still be Christians. He is not impressed by those who want to draw as near to sin as they can without actually sinning. Rather, God looks for those who diligently draw as near to Him as possible. He delights in those who are willing to refrain from things which may be harmless in order to direct more of their attention to Him.

God does have some basic minimum requirements for daily living. They are revealed in Micah 6:8: "He hath shewed thee, O man, what is good; and what doth the LORD require of thee, but to do justly, and to love mercy, and to walk humbly with thy God?"

1. To do justly. This means to act rightly, righteously, lawfully, and fairly. The Holy Bible contains 810,697 words, 31,175 verses, and 1,189 chapters. This first requirement is not a license to ignore a single one of these words. Every Word of God is essential (Matthew 4:4). It is a misinterpretation to say that this first requirement means God no longer requires obedience to His Word.

John F. Bettler gives an example of the false thinking on this subject even in religious circles:

In a recent interview with *Solo* magazine, Keith Miller said that Christians sometimes have to test God's ability to forgive by *going against what Scripture teaches.* Dealing with the question of remarriage after divorce in Matthew 19 he says, "I'm not trying to excuse divorce or say it's not wrong. I'm just saying that the God of the New Testament walking around in Jesus Christ was much bigger than the rules He gave. His actions showed again and again that He was bigger than the rules." Does that mean we can at times deliberately break the rules? Yes, says Miller, if you have big enough faith that Christ will forgive you anyway. Then, in reference to his own divorce he concludes, "I have, in fact, bet my spiritual life that this is true. In remarrying, I bet my life on Jesus Christ in a way I never did before. . . . Once in a while we've just got to jump those agonizing chasms in faith."

One does not judge Miller's personal agony or decision. But does he really believe that the church can prosper with such a shoddy hermeneutic? Does he not realize that he has put experiential judgment *above* Scripture? Has he never read Romans 6:1-2?[1]

Such an attitude is becoming increasingly widespread. It suggests that God is bigger than His rules, and that if we really love Him, we do not have to go by His Word all the time. But Jesus said, "If ye love me, keep my commandments" (John 14:15).

It is not true that if a person will just be sweet, act nice, and smile often, then he does not need to obey the Word of God. This belief is a replay of the tired old song from the Israelites: Everybody do what is right in his own eyes.

To do justly means, in the large, broad sense, to act in accordance with God's Word. We are incapable of determining what is just; only God can do that. The first requirement means, then, to find out what God's Word says and act according to it. The man who does so can be certain that he is acting justly.

(2) To love mercy. Mercy means kindness, benevolence and a forgiving spirit. It is directly linked to compassion, particularly compassion that is demonstrated by action, by involvement. (See Luke 10:37 and James 2:13.) God expects those who claim to love Him to demonstrate His love to others by getting actively involved, on a personal basis, with their hurts. God is not pleased with Christians who, with their hearts swelling in generosity, recommend that their hungry brothers check with the local food stamp outlet. He is not at all impressed with the concern demonstrated by those who help the needy family by placing a call to the Family Services Agency.

These attitudes, so prevalent in Christianity, are those of the priest and Levite, who passed by on the other side, refusing to dirty their hands with personal involvement.

The one who pleased the Lord in the parable was the Samaritan, who stopped, risked his own life, invested his own supplies and money, and personally transported the needy man to the inn. Neither did his concern stop there: he promised to pay the remainder of the bill upon his return.

Oppressive, heavy-handed bureaucracy is often the result of Christians' neglect of this second requirement. (See Proverbs 28:2.) The way to untangle that web is for Christians once again to take up their responsibilities.

3. To walk humbly. God hates pride. Seven things are an abomination to the Lord; the first is a proud look (Proverbs 6:16-17). God resists the proud, but He gives grace to the humble (James 4:6). Humility begins when a person realizes that God and other people are fully responsible for any good thing he possesses or has done. Pride begins when individuals take personal credit for these things. The glory must always be given to God. Christians are to live in such a way that people will see their good works but will give glory to God (Matthew 5:16). Pride takes the glory for itself; humility gives it all away.

These three requirements work together in a beautiful relationship for the advancement of God's kingdom. First, He wants a people who will obey Him. Then, those people are to put His Word into action, to demonstrate His love to others, thereby confronting them with the demonstration of the gospel. Finally, He wants those who obey and act to do so with humility.

Such a combination will result in a powerful, undeniable witness for our Lord.

Note

[1]Article in *Momentum,* Vol. 11, No. 2, a publication of The Christian Counselling and Educational Foundation.

17

"I Appeal Unto Caesar"

Some people have questioned the wisdom and prudence of the Apostle Paul's decision to go to Jerusalem and his decision to proclaim to Festus, "I appeal unto Caesar" (Acts 25:11). They reason that Paul was warned of the Holy Ghost of the sufferings that awaited him in Jerusalem so that he might be spared the difficulty, and that if he had not insisted on his legal rights in his appeal to a higher court he could have escaped lengthy incarceration and execution.

Such a view does not take into account Paul's tremendous spirituality, his extensive knowledge of the Word, and the reality of such scriptural truths as, "Yea, and all that will live godly in Christ Jesus shall suffer persecution" (II Timothy 3:12).

"The steps of a good man are ordered by the LORD" (Psalm 37:23). It is doubtful if any man could surpass the Apostle Paul in this regard. Surely the Lord ordered his steps. He was so sensitive to the Spirit that, on one occasion, he discerned that it was not God's will for him to preach the gospel in Bithynia at that time (Acts 16:7). It is unlikely that any New Testament figure meditated more earnestly on the Word of God, and the person who thus meditates will prosper in all that he does (Psalm 1:2-3).

Paul was no spiritual novice who barged ahead by immature bravado into places where angels would fear to tread; neither was he a political activist who grasped at imagined wrongs in an attempt to foment revolution. Instead, he was a stable, mature, Spirit-filled and Spirit-led Christian, who could confidently say to the Corinthians, "Be ye followers of me, even as I also am of Christ" (I Corinthians 11:1). In short, Paul did the right thing in going to Jerusalem, even in the face of certain persecution, and in appealing to Caesar for justice.

Paul's example is helpful for today's Christians, particularly those in atheistic countries and even those in such historic bastions of freedom as the United States of America. Christians must be willing to declare and practice the Word of God, even in the face of certain persecution, and if need be, Christians must be willing to pursue every legal channel available to them in their efforts to preserve religious freedom.

This does not mean purposefully looking for ways to transgress the civil law. Christians are to be obedient, law-abiding, tax-paying citizens who pray for their government and give thanks for their leaders. Their first allegiance, however, is to the Almighty God, who rules over the universe and who reveals His will in His Word. If and when obedience to men means disobedience to God, Christians must say with the Apostle Peter, "We ought to obey God rather than men" (Acts 5:29).

God's promise of deliverance does not mean that the believer will have no tribulation. Jesus said tribulation would come to His disciples (John 16:33). No Christian should expect to be exempt from the trial of his faith (I Peter 1:7).

The idea that Christians will be exempt from pressure fails in two ways. First, it overlooks the untold sufferings of many sincere Christians around the world right now. It dulls the consciousness of North American Christians implying that this six percent of the world's population are "special" because they live in a land of freedom and that they are somehow impervious to any significant loss of those freedoms. Second, this view fails to warn and prepare Christians of the possible loss of freedoms and to instruct them in scriptural responses in the face of such loss.

The Lord's coming is imminent, and Christians should look forward to it with anticipation. However, the lessons of the New Testament saints, the examples of the entire scope of Christian history, and the current experiences of the persecuted church in other lands all demonstrate the wisdom of preparation for any possibility.

Pressures already exist in North America that would restrict religious freedom. Sadly, many who profess to be born again, to say nothing of those who actually are, sit in silent complacence, unwilling to get personally involved in anything that does not immediately affect them.

If the Apostle Paul were here, he would not flinch from wading into the midst of certain persecution, as well as the misunderstanding of brethren, to declare the Word of God. Neither would he hesitate to appeal his case all the way to the Supreme Court, if necessary to preserve religious freedoms.

May God grant the modern church more people like the Apostle Paul.

18

Preaching:
Back to the Basics

"You've come a long way, Baby," proclaims an advertisement for a tobacco company, which equates progress with a woman's freedom to smoke its product publicly. No one would deny that "Baby" has indeed come a long way. The only question is whether the journey has been in the right direction.

Change is not always progress. In fact, spiritual change is only progress if it is in the direction of restoring the ancient paths. (See Isaiah 58:12.) In other words, the church is heading in the right direction only if it is drawing closer to biblical standards and practices.

One of the things that has "come a long way" in recent history is preaching. Many books are available to tell a minister how to preach, how to entertain the audience, and how to keep their attention. One recently published book lays out a strategy whereby a preacher can deliver his entire sermon in no more than five or ten minutes. According to the author, that is sufficient time to impart

God's Holy Word to His people.

Much that passes for preaching today resembles a Hollywood or Madison Avenue production more than a biblical message. From the lady evangelist of some years back who rode a motorcycle down the aisle of the auditorium, costumed as a policewoman, and who swung out over the congregation on a rope, to the modern emphasis on short, sweet, unoffensive sermons, preaching has been traveling down a fast road to nowhere.

The thunderings of an Isaiah or Jeremiah, the pointed finger of a Nathan, the steely eye of a John the Baptist, or the unwavering clarity of a Peter or Paul would be quite out of place in many of today's pulpits. Neither Peter nor Paul had too many animal stories to tell; John the Baptist did not use many illustrations to let the light in on his sermons.

Biblical preaching is not storytelling or lecturing or giving motivational seminars. The key is found in Paul's admonition to Timothy: "Preach the word; be instant in season, out of season; reprove, rebuke, exhort with all long-suffering and doctrine" (II Timothy 4:2).

The first obligation of the preacher is to preach the Word. There is a vast difference in preaching the Word and preaching about the Word. Too many preachers begin their sermon by reading one verse of Scripture and using it as a springboard for what they really want to say. Some actually feel that the difference between preaching and teaching is the amount of Scripture used. Perhaps if the minister reads less than five verses at the beginning of his message, it is preaching; if he reads more than five, it is teaching. This is, of course, nonsense. The recorded sermons in the Book of Acts consist largely of

Scripture quotations and applications from the Old Testament. As one venerable preacher has said, "We have too many sermonettes being preached by preacherettes to Christianettes."

In the Old Testament, it was the practice to spend the major part of a day in reading the Word to the people. In the New Testament, as Paul's sermon stretched out, one fellow in the window went to sleep and fell out of the second story to his death. Paul simply went down, raised him from the dead, and came back to continue his message.

There is nothing in the world more important than the Word of God. The preacher must always be ready to declare God's Word; he must be instant in season, out of season.

The second obligation of the preacher is to reprove. The word *reprove* means "to blame, to censure, to charge with a fault, to chide." This is not exactly what the pulpit committee is looking for when the new preacher is "trying out." (Where did that term ever come from?) So many want to hear something smooth and soothing, something that makes them feel better. Paul predicted as much: "For the time will come when they will not endure sound doctrine; but after their own lusts shall they heap to themselves teachers, having itching ears; and they shall turn away their ears from the truth, and shall be turned unto fables" (II Timothy 4:3-4).

The preacher's third obligation is to rebuke. In addition to some shades of meaning it has in common with *reprove,* this word means a preacher must "check or restrain, chasten, punish, afflict for correction, silence." Again, this task is not likely to make the preacher a prime

167

candidate for the Jaycee's Young Man of the Year. It may not motivate the mayor to come out with the key to the city. It may, instead, result in the preacher being let down in a basket over the wall.

The fourth obligation of the preacher is to exhort. At last we come to what most people would like to hear exclusively. Exhortation consists of giving strength, spirit, or courage by the spoken word. If the preacher tries to do this with anything other than God's Word, however, the people will be temporarily pumped up only to be deflated at the first sign of trouble.

The preacher must preach with longsuffering and doctrine. There is no place for the impatient man in the pulpit, and there is no place for a preacher who does not emphasize teaching (doctrine). A preacher must be able to continue declaring the Word with love, gentleness, wisdom and patience, even if progress seems miniscule. While he does not hesitate to declare the Word of the Lord firmly, neither does he throw up his hands in despair when not every member comes into perfect alignment with it overnight. He knows the responsibility for acting rests with the hearers.

When God's preachers proclaim His Word with longsuffering and doctrine, and when God's people obey the Word, then God's church will be victorious.